The Wisdom Tree

A Mother's Journey into Israel and the
Palestinian Territories

DIANE UMSTEAD

Finalist, 2011 Writers' League of Texas Manuscript Contest

ISBN: 0615698743
ISBN 13: 9780615698748
Library of Congress Control Number: 2012949438
The Wisdom Tree: A Mother's Journey into Israel and the Palestinian
Territories, Austin, TX

Map by Nick Springer.
Copyright © 2012 Springer Cartographics LLC

Wisdom is like a baobab: no-one can embrace it.

—*African proverb*

Contents

Map
vii

Bedouin Kidnappers
1

Consider This Area Off-Limits When Planning Your Itinerary
13

What is Hebrew for "Women's Restroom"?
29

The Future Population of Arad is Fifty Thousand
37

Welcome to the Lowest Spot on Earth
45

A Bedouin Disneyland
53

Dead Sea Perils and Positive Energies
65

Desert Survival Skills
73

The Salt Pillar of Lot's Wife
83

Go in Peace and Havahavahava Nice Day
89

Wisdom is Like a Baobab
99

Jerusalem, al-Quds
109

Here, of the Virgin Mary, Jesus Christ Was Born
119

Come and Celebrate Palestine
129

Closed Military Zones and Flying Checkpoints
143

Stink Water and Nasty Graffiti
153

Shabbat Desecraters Must Die!
169

Refugee Rappers
173

Thou Shalt Not Steal
183

The Sherut at Jaffa Gate
193

Postscript: Coyotes Howling at the Bloodmobile Door
199

Acknowledgements
205

Notes and Sources
207

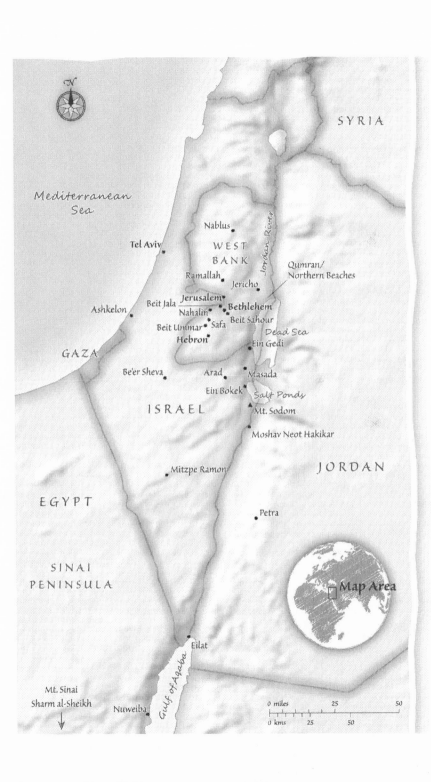

SYRIA

Mediterranean
Sea

Nablus

Tel Aviv

WEST
BANK

Jordan River

Qumran/
Northern Beaches

Ramallah

Jericho

Jerusalem

Beit Jala

Bethlehem

Ashkelon

Nahalin

Beit Sahour

Beit Ummar

Safa

Dead Sea

Hebron

Ein Gedi

GAZA

Be'er Sheva

Arad

Masada

Ein Bokek

Salt Ponds

ISRAEL

Mt. Sodom

Moshav Neot Hakikar

Mitzpe Ramon

JORDAN

Petra

EGYPT

SINAI
PENINSULA

Map Area

Eilat

Gulf of Aqaba

Mt. Sinai
Sharm al-Sheikh

Nuweiba

0 miles   25   50

0 kms   25   50

Few cars are on this stark strip of blacktop leading south to the Negev Desert. The sky is clear and blue, the air hot and dry. Terraced groves, low hills dotted with trees, and wheat-colored grasses of the coastal plains gradually give way to brown mounds of rock and dust. The young Israeli rental agent who programmed my navigation device at the airport said it is possible for a rocket launched from Gaza to hit this highway. "I'm setting this thing so you won't see any Arabs," he added with a smile. But this is no joke. My fingers ache from the tight grip I have on the steering wheel. What if I can't find Mark? What if I get lost? What if I'm abducted by Hamas militants? I glance east toward the West Bank, but see no signs of fighting, and then west toward Gaza, scanning for telltale flares in the sky, but see no rockets. More than an hour into the drive, at the northern edge of the Negev, the land is flat and strewn with jagged boulders, a desolate expanse with little sign of human habitation. The scorching desert air seeps into the compact car. The air conditioner slowly stops cooling. I feel my contact lenses crinkling in my eyes. I am parched.

Bedouin Kidnappers

Our son Mark is a climber. He always has been a climber, green eyes targeting the tallest tree, dark curls, followed by scrambling arms and legs, disappearing into leafy canopies. And when he fell (which, in truth, he rarely did), his father, Rex, and I were always there to catch him—that is, until he began traveling beyond our reach to conquer faraway summits like the limestone spires of El Potrero Chico and the sheer ice walls of Davidson Glacier.

It was Mark's boundless sense of adventure that led him to an assignment writing for the student-run travel guide *Let's Go* during the summer of 2009, before his senior year at Harvard. His work would take him to Egypt's Sinai Peninsula, Jordan's ancient city Petra, Israel's Negev Desert and Dead Sea, and the part of the Palestinian territories known as the West Bank. Not an Arab, not a Jew, and a stranger to that part of the world, Mark seemed a curious pick for the job. Perhaps he was hired because of his desert survival and wilderness training skills. Or maybe it was precisely because he was unfamiliar with the area and neither an Arab nor a Jew—a tabula rasa free of bias and prejudice. But Mark suspected he got the job because he was the only applicant who claimed to know how to drive a stick shift, a necessary skill when renting the cheapest of cars in the Middle East. Whatever the reason, he was thrilled with the prospect of spending eight weeks in foreign lands, writing about remote climbs, exotic foods, ancient monuments, and the least expensive hostels and campsites along the way.

Rex and I were delighted that Mark would actually have a paying job, but we were still apprehensive, especially about the time our son would spend working in the West Bank. What about terrorists and suicide bombers? Had it been so long since Rex and I, as young attorneys, believing we were immune to all danger, honeymooned in Kenya in the wake of the unrest following the military's aborted attempt to topple then-President Daniel arap Moi? We arrived just weeks after rebel groups in Africa had declared "open season" on foreigners and Kenyan gunmen had ambushed a tourist bus near Nairobi. We were intoxicated by the sense of adventure, undeterred by stories we'd heard along the way about kidnappings, massacres, and other atrocities. At this juncture, twenty-six years later, did I bear any resemblance to the young woman who (after Rex returned to Houston to prepare for a trial) spent several weeks backpacking alone in Europe on the "second leg of our honeymoon"? Where were these fearless individuals? Had parenthood altered us at such a cellular level? Apparently it had.

We checked the State Department's website:

THE DEPARTMENT OF STATE URGES U.S.
CITIZENS TO DEFER TRAVEL
TO THE WEST BANK AT THIS TIME.

I was indignant. How could the editors of *Let's Go* send Mark to the West Bank? Had they not read the State Department's warning? Mark's girlfriend, Beryl, also hired to write for the guidebook, would spend her summer in Florence, Italy. Beryl was going to the city of Botticelli and Valentino. Mark was going to a war zone.

On Saturday, May 23, the day after spring-term exams ended, Mark packed all he would need for his two-month assignment into one backpack and bundled everything else off to storage—all the clothes, books, posters, and musical instruments he had moved over the preceding three years from our home in Austin, Texas, to his dorm in Cambridge, Massachusetts. That afternoon, he perfected his stick-shift skills at the official *Let's Go* driver training course. And less than twenty-four hours later, he was on his way to London, where he would spend a day sightseeing with Beryl before they each boarded a connecting flight to their final destinations. Mark managed all of this alone. He flew across the world without my having tucked a single item into his suitcase, without a final hug from his mother before boarding his flight. He was, after all, twenty-one years old. I hoped he'd done the "idiot check," the one last look under beds and in closets to make sure he'd left nothing essential behind before leaving the dorm. It was a ritual Rex had instilled in Mark and our younger son, Paul, from their childhoods.

Mark apparently took everything he needed to get on his flights. He emailed when he arrived in Israel: "Free wifi in the Tel Aviv airport. I love this country already. Seems to be an attitude that the only way to beat the extremists is to embrace global capitalism and become as cosmopolitan as possible. The bus company website is in Hebrew, so I'll buy a phone card and call to find out when the next bus leaves for Eilat." Searching a map of the Middle East that I kept with a copy of Mark's itinerary in the top drawer of my desk, I located Eilat at the very southern tip of Israel, bordering the Gulf of Aqaba. It would be a two-hundred-mile bus ride from the airport and through the Negev Desert to Eilat.

Mark emailed again once settled at a youth hostel in Eilat, extolling the city's "amazing beaches and good nightlife." The town, he discovered, was a tourist haven for twenty-somethings: scuba diving, snorkeling, and sunbathing during the day, club-hopping and dancing after dark. I could tell he was enjoying himself, and his assignment sounded no more hazardous than the typical spring-break vacation. I began to think that his job wasn't so ill considered after all. Perhaps it would be the Kerouacian adventure he'd dreamed of while writing his high-school senior paper about the author. Sans the debauchery, I hoped.

While in Eilat, Mark sent us an occasional "I'm alive" email and called once or twice. Here in Austin and long removed from my days negotiating travel while honeymooning in Kenya, my biggest life challenge was a troublesome bathroom remodeling job, which kept me from dwelling full time on the hazards of Mark's job. But when several consecutive days passed without a word from our son, I started to dwell. I dug out his *Let's Go* itinerary from my desk drawer and began matching the dates and times with his likely whereabouts. This week, having completed his assignment in Eilat, he was scheduled to be in the Sinai Peninsula of Egypt. I searched online for news from Egypt. Most of the coverage focused on President Obama's upcoming trip to the country. The Egyptian government was stepping up security around Cairo, where our president would be delivering a speech to the Arab world. With Obama on his way to Egypt, I reasoned that it was a pretty safe place, even if the government's enhanced precautions didn't extend all the way to the remote spots in the southeastern Sinai Peninsula where Mark was working.

If the news from Egypt was somewhat encouraging, the dispatches from Israel and the Palestinian territories were not. While Mark had been in Cambridge popping gears in his *Let's Go* driver training course, and while I had been pacing the aisles of Ferguson's Plumbing Supply debating the merits of nickel versus stainless steel faucets, there'd been fighting in Israel and the Palestinian territories. Near Gaza, Israeli soldiers killed two heavily armed Islamic extremists caught planting an explosive near the border fence. Hours later, at a different section of the fence, a bomb exploded near an Israeli patrol vehicle. In the West Bank, there were clashes between the two Palestinian factions: Hamas, the militant faction, and Fatah, the mainstream group that is internationally recognized as representing the Palestinian people. Six people died near Nablus when Hamas militants threw a grenade at Fatah security patrols and Fatah patrols responded by storming the Hamas hideout. On the outskirts of Hebron, Israeli forces killed a Hamas militant believed to be responsible for two suicide bombings. I focused my attention on Mark's itinerary and the Middle East map. Gaza, where Islamic militants were planting bombs, was very close to several towns on Mark's upcoming itinerary. The Palestinian cities Nablus and Hebron, both sites of recent fighting, were both on Mark's work schedule. How could so much highly relevant news have escaped my notice?

As my concern mounted, I cursed *Let's Go* for giving Mark such a lousy assignment. I called Mark's cell phone, which was inexplicably and repeatedly answered by an Egyptian service provider in Arabic. I then launched a barrage of emails hoping to get his attention and alert him to all the dangers I'd uncovered. And to make certain that I wouldn't overlook any more important news from the places on Mark's itinerary, I signed up for *New York Times* email alerts for news covering those areas. Meanwhile, Rex remained calm, offering vague assurances like "Mark is independent and resourceful, and if he needs our help, he'll call." Was this a facade in order to appear strong for my benefit? Was Rex burying his own feelings in an attempt to conquer his own rising fear? I hoped his confidence was justified.

Then, a day or so later, an email from Mark lit up my inbox: "Sorry to drop off the map like that. Call me whenever you want. It would be great to talk to you!" Had he not seen my emails about our inability to get through on his phone? After several attempts, Rex and I reached Mark. He had been busy, he said. He had taken a midnight climb up Mt. Sinai, where he sat through the night on an outcropping of rock at the summit and watched the sunrise. From Mt. Sinai, he had traveled by bus to Sharm al-Sheikh, an Egyptian tourist destination bordering the Gulf of Aqaba, where he'd checked out scuba diving outfitters and interviewed local people to see what else he might write about. Yes, he'd heard a little about some violence, but this was the Middle East. Hoping Mark would remain vigilant and sensing that he wasn't in any immediate danger, I finally felt free to leave home for something other than groceries and plumbing supplies.

Several days later, Rex and I returned home from an early morning bicycle ride to find a phone voice message from Mark:

"CALL ME! SOME BEDOUINS HAVE ME LOCKED IN A ROOM. ONE HAS AN AK-47!"

I do not believe we were breathing as we dialed Mark's number. AK-47? Bedouin kidnappers? Bedouins—the nomads with tents and camels? I remembered them from my childhood in Libya. My father, a fighter pilot with the US Air Force's 431st Fighter-Interceptor Squadron, a group of hotshot aviators who called themselves the Red Devils, was stationed at Wheelus Field in Tripoli. Our Mediterranean-style concrete duplex sat at the very edge of the rocky land that extended to the Sahara Desert. One morning my mother, sisters, and I spotted camels, necks arched over our back wall, chewing on sheets from our clothesline. Unfamiliar goats grazed on patches of fragile grass, recently sprouted from Sears Roebuck seeds, in our otherwise barren yard. Through the back gate we saw newly erected tents and a contingent of Bedouins in white turbans who gazed enigmatically back at us. I remember the Bedouins, but I never dreamed of Bedouin kidnappers!

Still no phone connection. The seemingly endless hissing and static finally gave way to ringing and, at last, Mark's voice. "Mom . . . Dad! I just got out of the room! I started banging on the door and they let me out! Salah said he stuck a spoon in the door latch to keep the door closed!"

Mark interrupted our frantic queries. "I met this Bedouin, Salah Mohammed. His family owns a beach camp south of Nuweiba, and it sounded like something I could write about for *Let's Go*. The camp is just one small building with a kitchen and a room above it that they rent out. The Bedouins sleep on the beach."

Mark went on to explain. Salah had shown him to the room above the kitchen. On the way upstairs, Salah had mentioned that he hunted ibex with an AK-47, and he'd also commented that he liked Mark's cargo shorts—a pronounced contrast to the long-sleeved white shirts extending to the ground that the Bedouin men and boys wore. Salah had gone back downstairs while Mark unpacked, but when Mark tried to leave he discovered the door had been locked from the outside. He realized he was trapped in a room somewhere in the Sinai and no one knew where he was. "I started to wonder if Salah might kill me for my cargo shorts, and that's when I left the message for you. But when I started banging on the door, Salah came right up and opened it." Mark tried to reassure us that he no longer felt threatened. "Salah told me that he and his cousin are going to take their boat out tonight to catch a fish for dinner."

Rex and I weren't so sure. What if Salah did have plans to kidnap Mark, or worse? While still on the phone with Mark, we suggested a plan: He could tell Salah he had to return to Nuweiba to do some research for *Let's Go*. Once he was safe in Nuweiba, Mark could check into a hotel and never return to the beach camp.

Mark was reluctant. "Salah and his family are already planning dinner for me. I can't just pick up and leave." He suggested an alternative: He would tell Salah he had to return to Nuweiba for a few hours to do research. Once there, he would check into a hotel and then take a taxicab back to Salah's camp to eat dinner while the cab waited nearby. After dinner, Mark would tell Salah he had to return to Nuweiba to finish his work for *Let's Go*, and Mark would get in the cab and leave the camp for good.

The plan of action set, Mark said he would call us later that evening from the hotel in Nuweiba.

Rex and I stationed ourselves in our kitchen all afternoon, answering the phone on the first ring and quickly terminating all calls the moment it was clear that the caller wasn't Mark. We pored over maps of Egypt to pinpoint Mark's exact location, searched the Internet for information on Bedouin beach camps in the Sinai Peninsula, and levied further curses against *Let's Go* for giving our son such a treacherous assignment.

Just after six o'clock in the evening in Austin (well after midnight in Egypt), Mark called from his hotel room in Nuweiba. He spoke in the rapid-fire, pause-free way that always rendered his excitement obvious. "Salah and his cousin took their boat out and caught a huge fish. They boiled it in a pot without any spices, because they don't have any spices. Salah's mother heated stones to cook bread, which was flat and charred. We sat on rocks on the beach and ate. It was one of the best meals I've ever had!" Breath. Mark felt guilty about thinking Salah might kill him and about rushing off right after dinner. But with the cab waiting and most of his things already at the hotel, Mark had to leave. He thanked the entire family for dinner and retrieved the rest of the gear he had left upstairs—the things he'd left behind earlier to prevent

9

Salah from suspecting he'd left for good. As a parting gift, Mark left his cargo shorts in the room for Salah.

With Mark securely sheltered in his hotel for the night, Rex and I consumed a bottle of wine, replayed the details of the Bedouins and Mark's predicament, and felt comforted that our son had escaped a potentially lethal situation. We slept well that night.

The next morning, Mark called from his hotel room in Nuweiba to report that his wallet had been stolen from the room during the night.

We wired money to Mark through a bank in Eilat, where he said he'd be spending one day between his work in Egypt and Jordan. It was enough to help him get by until he could arrange for a new credit card. Bank of America, it turned out, was a little uneasy about sending a new card directly to him in the Middle East. That afternoon, he emailed to thank us for the money and let us know he was on his way to Jordan.

When Mark first got the job with *Let's Go*, Rex and I had discussed taking a summer trip to Egypt or Israel to see him. And while confined to the house for extended periods awaiting plumbers and electricians, I'd even browsed possible vacation destinations and flight schedules. The previous day's mishaps prompted another discussion about our going to the Middle East. But now Rex was committed to a father-son trip to Alaska to celebrate Paul's high school graduation. It would be three weeks before Rex could make the trip to the Middle East. If I wanted to go sooner, I'd have to go alone.

While waiting to hear from Mark, I continued to closely monitor my email alerts from the *New York Times*. In the previous few days, Israeli soldiers near Ramallah killed a Palestinian man who was participating in a demonstration against Israel's construction of the Separation Wall between Israel and the West Bank, and Israeli forces near Gaza killed four of ten Palestinian gunmen who were spotted wearing and planting explosive devices along the Israel-Gaza border fence. Again, I checked Mark's itinerary and the Middle East map. In a few weeks, Mark would be working in Ramallah; this week he'd be working in several towns in the Negev Desert, within rocket-striking distance of Gaza.

Mark resurfaced a few days later in one of those Negev towns, Mitzpe Ramon, where he called home to tell us about his trip to Jordan. He said he'd sprinted the narrow, mile-long crevice between the soaring cliffs of Petra's main entrance to the ancient remains of the Roman city, where rust-colored sandstone mountains had been carved to create a treasury building, a theater, and other elaborately detailed structures he'd first seen in *Indiana Jones and the Last Crusade*. In the midst of the ruins, he encountered an old Bedouin with a wooden teacart. More Jack Sparrow than Indiana Jones, the peddler wore his long black hair twined with, as Mark put it, "colored strings and six or more bandanas." Mark spent the afternoon with the tea peddler, drinking tea laced with cardamom and sage and watching the Roman amphitheater glow a blazing white, then ember-red in the evolving light of evening. From Jordan, Mark made his way to Mitzpe Ramon on a bus filled to capacity with Israeli Defense Forces recruits, all with cleanly shaven heads, fatigues, and assault rifles.

In Mitzpe Ramon, Mark abandoned his plan to stay in a hostel and was sleeping in an old industrial hangar. The hangar stood at the edge of town in a stretch of desert scattered with

abandoned buildings, several of which had been co-opted by artists. This one had been converted into a dance studio, but it was
unused at night and the owners let Mark sleep on a yoga mat on
the floor. This arrangement was a lot less expensive than staying
in a hostel, perfect for a frugal *Let's Go* traveler. From the hangar
he could scout out desert trails and mountain hikes and catch the
morning bus to explore other Negev towns to gather information
for the travel guide. To save money on food, he cooked cans of
beans for dinner outside over an open campfire.

Mark had heard nothing about the Palestinian gunmen planting
explosive devices along the Gaza border north of Mitzpe Ramon,
though he did say he thought he'd seen some "military activity" in
the desert not far from the hangar. He speculated the area might be
a training ground for the Israeli Defense Forces. Nonetheless, Mark
assured us that he felt safe staying in the hangar, though with some
prodding, he admitted that it was a little eerie alone at night. Desert
winds pummeled the cavernous structure, making the huge doors
clank, the sides creak, and the roof threaten to blow off.

Later that same evening, Rex and I hosted a party at our house
to welcome one of his law firm's new partners. I normally enjoy
these sorts of affairs, but that night my thoughts were elsewhere.
I pictured my son alone in the hangar with the desert winds howling and the massive metal doors clattering open and creaking shut.
I could see him sleeping peacefully on his yoga mat while in the
desert nearby Israeli Defense Forces planned military strikes on
Gaza, and sixty miles to the north, Palestinian gunmen from Gaza
planted explosives along the border.

My only thought was, *I can't get to the Middle East soon enough!*

Consider This Area
Off-Limits When Planning
Your Itinerary

It had been just a day since Mark called from his makeshift quarters in the industrial hangar in the Negev. I imagined myself taking off for Tel Aviv, making my way through the inhospitable desert landscape, and finding my son. Together, in some civilized locale, we would track down a small hotel out of harm's way and with very good coffee. I decided to make the trip soon. There was no way I could wait for Rex and Paul to return from their upcoming expedition to Alaska. I announced my plans to Rex, who agreed that it was a good idea.

I called Mark. Though it was after midnight on his side of the planet, he was stretched out on a heap of yoga mats reading *Herzog* by flashlight in the dark hangar. He sounded relaxed and pleased to hear my voice. My mind raced as I simultaneously listened to his account of his day and to my inner voices scrolling through all the dangers I'd imagined. From his base camp at Mitzpe Ramon, Mark had mountain biked to the rim of a vast crater, Makhtesh Ramon. And from the crater's edge, he had gingerly descended a decaying rope ladder into the depths of the giant cavity and hiked alone along geological formations that looked like the landscape of an alien planet. A squadron of Israeli fighter jets flew in a low formation over the lip of the crater as he watched from below.

For his evening meal, he managed a dinner of pasta, which he boiled in a tin can over his campfire. He laughed as he recounted his return to the industrial hangar after dark, with his hair and clothes saturated with smoke. There was a dance performance in process. Barely clothed dancers gleaming with scented oils were suspended from the ceiling on ropes. "So I sit down with the audience like I'd been invited, and people start turning around to find the smoky smell. After everyone left, I went to the bathroom to brush my teeth and saw that I had black ashes smeared all over my face. I can't imagine what those people thought when they turned around and saw me sitting there!" We were both really laughing now. However, the thought of Mark with his soot-streaked face made me think of desert camouflage, which, in turn, led me to imagine terrorists and how he was still alone and defenseless in the desert, cooking food in rusty old cans over an open fire. Back to the original and overriding purpose of my phone call—how could I suggest that I join him in Israel without looking as though I wanted to check up on him or, perish the thought, rescue him?

In my most nonchalant voice, doing my best not to appear to be "checking up" on him, I told Mark about my plans to travel to Israel for a couple of weeks while Rex and Paul were in Alaska. He and I could spend some time together when he was not working, and I'd entertain myself when he was.

Without hesitation, Mark said that would be "cool," that he'd love to show me around. He suggested I take a flight that would get me to Israel the following week, and that I meet him in Arad, a small town at the intersection of the Negev Desert and the Judean Hills. From Arad, we would drive east to the coastal area along the Dead Sea, where he would be working for a week or so. After that, we'd go on to the West Bank.

I was elated by his response, terrified by our itinerary. While the "Dead Sea" evoked visions of spa treatments and sunbathing, the "West Bank" sounded more akin to a bad-news day on CNN.

That evening, putting my fears aside, I began my search for flights from Austin to Israel. Should I fly El Al Airlines ("It's not just an airline, it's Israel") or Continental Airlines, based in nearby Houston? I decided against El Al, a likely flying target for anti-Israeli terrorists (though much later I discovered it has a near perfect safety record because of its stringent security measures). I booked a Continental flight that would depart the following week and arrive in Israel early in the morning. This would give me time to travel to the Negev before dark to meet Mark.

Having finalized my plane reservations, I devoted several days to wrapping up the bathroom remodeling project before turning to the other logistics of my trip. Between plumbing inspections and the like, I continued to monitor news from the Middle East. In the last few days, Palestinian militants had fired a *Qassam* rocket (a type of homemade projectile) from Gaza into the Ashkelon Beach area of Israel. The Israeli military retaliated by attacking two tunnels under the Gaza-Egypt border. Hamas, the Palestinian party controlling Gaza, declared that the tunnels were a vital means of importing food and supplies because Israel had sealed off the Gaza-Israel and Gaza-Egypt border crossings, whereas Israel claimed that the tunnels were used to transport banned weapons. After the Israeli attack, Palestinian militants fired a second Qassam rocket from Gaza into Israel's Ashkelon Beach area.

Meanwhile, Rex, Paul, and I communicated with Mark by email and Skype, as his Egyptian phone was no longer in service. Mark had been working in several desert towns, including Sdeh Boker, Dimona, and Mamshit (a name that made us all laugh), and in the Negev's largest city, Be'er Sheva. He'd sprung for two nights at a youth hostel in Be'er Sheva, but at forty dollars a night, he concluded it was "an unaffordable luxury." So, he was once again staying in the industrial hangar in Mitzpe Ramon at night and taking the fifty-mile bus trip each morning to research Be'er Sheva and other areas on his itinerary.

With all home projects at a stopping point, I turned my attention to my quickly approaching trip. How would I get around the country? Mark had been traveling mostly by bus but suggested I consider renting a car at the airport because there was not a direct bus to Arad. I found a road map of Israel and with my finger traced the series of roads that would get me from Tel Aviv to Arad. The undulating red line on the map led me directly between the two Palestinian territories—Gaza and the West Bank. This was not at all the route I had hoped for. I checked the map of Israel to find "Ashkelon," the target of recent rocket strikes. It was less than fifteen miles from the north-south highway that would lead me from the airport to Arad. I decided that I needed to talk to someone with experience driving in Israel.

My sister Sheri and her husband, Grant, had two things I deemed absolutely necessary right now: a willingness to jump into any situation with practical advice, and a friend who had moved with his family to Israel several years ago. I hadn't seen Chaim for ten years or so but remembered that he had once been the captain of his college tennis team and was still, in his mid-fifties, rather debonair. Sheri and Grant helped me track him down in Israel by email. Would he even remember me? Chaim responded graciously to my long and fretful email: "We moved to Israel, but we don't have amnesia. We remember you fondly." He assured me that Israel was a very "with it" and visitor-friendly place. "Everybody in Israel speaks English . . . or someone right next to them does. People are very helpful here." Though he wouldn't be in Israel when my plane arrived, Chaim offered "remote assistance" if needed. He also recommended that I rent a car with a navigation device, which would give me more flexibility than taking a bus. He said it was perfectly safe to drive a car in Israel. Had he been reading the news? Was Chaim using his innate charm to "sell" Israel to this wary tourist? But, obviously, people do drive in Israel; I would take his advice about the car.

As for accommodations, I asked Chaim about the Ein Gedi Kibbutz, which I'd read about online. It was set on a plateau overlooking the Dead Sea, near where Mark would be working the first week I was in Israel, and to my surprise, it operated a guesthouse with a restaurant, bar, and swimming pool, completely incongruous with my mental image of a kibbutz. "Ein Gedi is enormously famous for its gardens, geology, and freshwater springs right in the middle of the Judean Desert," Chaim emailed. "The accommodations are sparse, but totally acceptable."

Then I asked Chaim about the West Bank. He said he had driven there, but because he is Jewish he could only travel to certain areas: "Area A is run by the Palestinians and is out of bounds for me—I am not allowed to travel there, and would not. If you want to go to Area A, and you are Jewish, or Israeli, you (1) can't and (2) would have to be insane to try. It is strictly verboten and dangerous!"

Area A? I hadn't heard anything about Area A until Chaim mentioned it. I was, however, somewhat familiar with many details of the circumstances surrounding the creation of Israel and the ensuing struggle between the Jews and Arabs. In the months before this trip unexpectedly leapt onto my agenda, I had been thoroughly absorbed in a series of articles with firsthand news accounts from Israel's turbulent beginnings. At the time, Mark was away at college and Paul was taking a gap year (during which he hoped to be gainfully employed) between high school and college. With neither son needing much of my attention, I found myself with more time to pursue other interests. One of those interests was Libya, the country in which I was born while my father was stationed near Tripoli. Curiosity led to full-scale research and my discovering the microfilm archives of the *Sunday Ghibli*, a newspaper published in Tripoli by the British Military Administration after World War II. (Following the war, both British and US forces, having defeated the Italian and German armies in northern Africa and elsewhere, maintained a presence in Tripoli.) As it turned out, a good part of Paul's gap-year experience involved sporadic seasonal work, like walking the streets for the US Census Bureau and registering voters for Travis County. He spent many hours sitting on the couch in his boxers, studying probability tables, reading Sklansky and Malmuth on poker theory, and playing Texas Hold 'em online—his plan for earning cash without having to work nine to five. My time as a lawyer in a large Houston firm taught me how to delegate, and here was the perfect job for Paul. Off he went with a shoebox of microfilm to the Austin public library, where he became a master operator of the library's new microfilm printing machine, threading thin filmstrips through the projector and making copies of each page of every newspaper. It was a challenging project. The microfilm newspaper pages were too large to print on one letter-sized piece of copy paper, so Paul divided each microfilm page into quadrants and positioned the projector by hand to get a shot of individual quadrants. For several months, he spent his days with his six-foot-three body bent and hovering over the library's microfilm machine and his evenings, before settling in with his poker books, recounting stories he'd read while making copies. Paul found the natural disasters particularly engaging. The worst *ghibli* (sandstorm) that ever struck Tripoli blanketed the entire city with hot, swirling sand that poured into the cracks and crevices of houses "like warm water into a bottle" and brought life to a standstill for days. Another article provided details of an invasion staged by locust hoppers that swarmed over the plains south of Tripoli and marched like an army "on a front seventeen kilometers wide and three kilometers deep." Local tribesmen ultimately defeated and destroyed the insect armies, with the help of British and American troops.

Paul's copying job began with the issues of the *Sunday Ghibli* published in 1948. Although my father was then a cadet at West Point and our family didn't arrive in Tripoli until 1953, I was interested in the 1948 news reports about British and American efforts to create a government in Libya that was friendly to the West. It was in these newspapers that I came across articles about the creation of another government, one for the national administration of Palestine. The United Nations General Assembly voted in November of 1947 to partition Palestine into two states—one for Arabs and one for Jews—to come into existence no later than October 1, 1948, with Jerusalem and Bethlehem to be internationally administered cities. Although Jews comprised less than a third of the population and held legal title to only 7 percent of the land in Palestine, the UN plan stipulated that more than 54 percent of the land in Palestine would go to the new Jewish state. Most Arabs were angered by the plan and opposed the partition. Even if from another era, the implications felt bleak. Seemingly without a break in the chronology, headline followed headline: "Strife Continues in Palestine," "Still More Palestine Outrages," "No Let Up in Reign of Lawlessness." I had to pause often to absorb the constant flow of "violence, murder, and arson" that followed the UN plan to partition Palestine. On January 4, 1948, the *Sunday Ghibli* reported:

> In Palestine throughout the Christmas period and into the new year the crazy, wicked business of communal strife continued, as the vicious circle of feud and revenge took its steadily mounting toll of human life, Jew, Arab, and British. . . . Since the United Nations made the decision to partition the country, there has been a gradual spread of violence throughout the country with heavy loss of life.

The British, who had been administering affairs in Palestine since the defeat of the Turks and the collapse of the Ottoman Empire in World War I, found themselves in the crossfire from both sides, Arabs and Jews.

The turmoil that followed the UN vote to partition Palestine escalated into a full-blown war between the Arabs and Jews. On May 16, 1948, in the midst of the fighting, the *Sunday Ghibli* announced the British withdrawal from Palestine in an article titled "Palestine Mandate Ends, 25 Years of British Achievement," which detailed how the British had turned the once "poor and undeveloped country" into "the most prosperous country in the Middle East." The paper also reported that the Jews had proclaimed the creation of the state of Israel:

> The birth of a Jewish State in Palestine to be called Israel was proclaimed in Tel Aviv on Friday afternoon at a solemn assembly of the Jewish National Council. They declared that the Jewish National State was being declared by virtue of natural and historic right of the Jewish people, and by resolution of the General Assembly of the United Nations.

The Arabs refused to recognize the existence of the state of Israel, as did Britain and other countries, and in the weeks following, the paper reported ongoing fighting between Arabs and Jews in Palestine.

On June 13, 1948, the *Sunday Ghibli* proclaimed, "Peace Returns to Palestine, UNO Truce Terms Accepted." The UN-appointed mediator, Count Folke Bernadotte, who had been traveling between

Arabs and Jews, had successfully negotiated a ceasefire, the paper reported. Arabs were encouraged because Bernadotte would be formulating an entirely new plan for Palestine, which if agreed to by both sides, would supersede the former UN partition plan. The encouragement was short-lived. On September 19, 1948, the *Sunday Ghibli* reported, "United Nations Mediator Murdered in Palestine, Dastardly Crime Shocks the World." Bernadotte, who was visiting Jerusalem for the last time before leaving the Middle East to attend UN Palestine discussions in Europe, was driving with his party through a Jewish-held area of the city when four men drove up in a jeep and one shot Bernadotte; the men were believed to be members of the militant Zionist Stern Group. (The Stern Group, also known as the Lehi Group, was headed by Yitzhak Shamir, who later served as Israel's prime minister.)

Although I was engrossed by the *Ghibli's* news accounts of the UN partition plan and its aftermath, at the time of my research I had never imagined that I would be flying off to Israel on my own personal mission. But now, with my trip to Israel just days away, I felt a deep, instinctive need to learn what had happened in the area since those decades-old news reports and to find out about Area A, the Palestinian-controlled area that Chaim mentioned in his email to me. I set out to do more research.

I learned that the 1948 Arab-Israeli War officially ended with the 1949 Armistice Agreements between Israel and neighboring Arab countries, which finalized the line partitioning Palestine. The new line, called the "Green Line," which was accepted by all parties to the agreement and confirmed as legal by the international community, gave Israel not only the land originally designated by the United

Nations for a future Jewish state, but also part of the land designated for the Arab state (about 77 percent of the land in Palestine). Jordan annexed the West Bank (about 22 percent of the land in Palestine), and Egypt took control of Gaza (about 1 percent of Palestine).

During the 1967 Six-Day War, Israel captured the Gaza Strip and the Sinai Peninsula from Egypt and the West Bank from Jordan. Israel pulled out of the Sinai in 1979, but continued occupying Gaza and the West Bank (the "Palestinian territories"), despite the UN Security Council's call for Israel's withdrawal from the Palestinian territories.

Between 1993 and 1995, Israeli and Palestinian representatives entered into several agreements, together called the Oslo Accords. These agreements established a self-governing body, called the Palestinian Authority, for Palestinians in Gaza and the West Bank, and set out guidelines and schedules for the withdrawal of Israeli forces from Palestinian-populated areas and for Palestinian self-rule. The plan divided the Palestinian territories into three areas, each with distinctive rules for security and administration:

> Area A—Palestinian Authority control over internal security, public order, and civil affairs in Gaza and the West Bank cities Ramallah, Bethlehem, Jericho, Nablus, Jenin, Kalkilya, and Tulkarem (Hebron was included later, under a separate agreement)
>
> Area B—Palestinian Authority control over public order and civil affairs in four hundred fifty Palestinian towns and villages in the West Bank; Palestinian control over internal security to be phased in, but Israel to retain overriding control over security for purposes of protecting Israelis and fighting terrorism

Area C—Israel military control and civil administration of all areas not included in Areas A and B; Palestinian control over civil affairs (unrelated to land) of Palestinians living in Area C

These interim arrangements set out by the Oslo Accords remain in place to this day because Israel and the Palestinians have failed to negotiate a permanent peace agreement.

Back to the logistics of my trip, I quickly scanned Mark's itinerary for the West Bank. Among other places, he would be working in Hebron, Ramallah, Bethlehem, Jericho, and Nablus—all designated Area A. Chaim had not been able to give me further advice about traveling in these Palestinian-controlled areas, other than "non-Jewish tourists do go to these places without incident" and "a US passport is magical, but not foolproof." Really? Though I trusted him, he had never actually traveled in the Palestinian-controlled areas.

On my route of preflight errands, I stopped by BookStop and flipped through shelves of guidebooks. There wasn't a current *Let's Go* guidebook for Israel, which was why Mark was assigned to update it. But I found several others, and they confirmed my worst fears. The *Frommer's* guide omitted the entire section on the Palestinian territories, and its advice to "consider this area off-limits when planning your itinerary" served only to ratchet up my anxiety. *Fodor's* was, at least, more descriptive: "Two well-supported, well-funded and well-armed Palestinian guerilla organizations are at war with Israel: Hamas and Islamic Jihad. Their presence in the West Bank makes it dangerous to travel there." A third guidebook, *Lonely Planet,* had a very lengthy section on the West Bank, but at the outset its writers warned, "Check news reports, ask authorities for the official line on travel to the West Bank, contact agencies in the region, and find out what church groups are doing. . . . Curfews, closures, roadblocks and military engagement can occur as soon as tensions arise."

As for driving a car in the West Bank, the authors of *Fodor's* spoke directly to my worst fears: "The stoning of cars with Israeli license plates (including rental cars) is common place. Shootings have also taken place, resulting in the deaths of numerous drivers and passengers." *Lonely Planet's* authors suggested that when driving in the West Bank, one should take certain precautions. For example, when in Palestinian-controlled areas it's best to look like a Palestinian sympathizer: "To avert the rare occurrence of a stone lobbed at your car, avoid appearing to be a religious Jew or a Jewish settler. Place a *keffiyeh* (a scarf like that worn by Arafat) on the dash. (A red one is also welcome, indicating a leftward leaning.) Remove it when stopped at a checkpoint as it could become an inadvertent conversation piece for bored Israeli soldiers." Probably good advice. Where does one purchase a red keffiyeh? It all made me wonder whether I should be driving a car in the West Bank at all.

Contemplating further, I concluded that traveling in the West Bank was a thoroughly bad idea. There was not one single travel guide that vouched for its safety. More than anything, I wanted to tell Mark so and tell him we shouldn't go. But I knew he had to go to the West Bank to complete his work for *Let's Go*. So, for now, I'd back off. When he eagerly explained how he would show me the West Bank during that part of his assignment, I would swallow the words that consumed my thoughts, "No! You can't go there! It's not safe! *Frommer's* says *no, no, no,* you cannot go," and I'd say instead, "Oh, yes, Mark, that sounds great." Once there, if I discovered that the area was fraught with danger or that Mark and I were likely to be captured or tortured or blown up by suicide bombers, I'd count on my maternal instincts to keep him safe.

In the midst of my fretting about my own trip, Rex and Paul set off on theirs. Having packed the car with their filled-to-capacity nylon backpacks, collapsible aluminum walking sticks, waterproof hiking boots, and other things they'd need for the ten-day trip, they departed Austin on Saturday, June 20, and drove to Dallas to catch a morning flight to Juneau, Alaska. From there, they would fly on a puddle jumper called "Wings of Alaska" to Skagway, where they would meet the Packer Expeditions guide who would accompany them on the Chilkoot Trail part of their trip. The thirty-three-mile trail, which would take them through the Coast Mountains of Alaska to the Yukon Territory of British Columbia, was the same route taken by prospectors during the 1890s Klondike Gold Rush. (Rex and Paul had been training for this strenuous trek for the past several weeks, stuffing their backpacks with anything bulky and conveniently located in our garage, like bottles of Clorox and boxes of shotgun shells, and hiking to downtown Austin and back; I thanked my lucky stars that Austin was not a focal point of Homeland Security scrutiny.) Rex assured me that he and Paul were in good hands with Packer Expeditions. The outfitter had top-of-line tents and other gear, he said, as well as some of the most experienced guides. The name "Packer," however, he considered "a little worrisome." The name came from the American gold prospector Alfred Packer, who in the late 1800s cannibalized his companions when their expedition became snowbound in the Rocky Mountains. Rex said he was hopeful that the same ethic did not apply to the twenty-first-century version of Packer Expeditions.

Because Rex and Paul wouldn't be reachable by phone while in the wilderness of Alaska and British Columbia, they called Mark before leaving our home in Austin. Mark offered them some advice about the Chilkoot Trail, which he'd hiked with friends a few years earlier: "Stay at least a hundred yards apart after you cross Chilkoot Pass so an avalanche doesn't bury both of you." Rex in turn gave Mark some fatherly advice, "Please take good care of your mom."

Once Rex and Paul were on their way, I began checking the final items off my to-do list: printing driving directions from the Tel Aviv airport to Arad, buying an iPhone and entering all of my rental confirmations, and packing the one carry-on suitcase that I'd take with me. When I reserved a car, I learned that Israeli car rental agencies do not supply navigation devices, so just in case I couldn't find one on arrival, I carefully planned the route I would drive. My drive would begin at the Tel Aviv airport, which I discovered isn't actually in Tel Aviv. I was relieved to bypass the congested streets of that city, a huge metropolis and the largest city in Israel. The airport was closer to Lod, a town southeast of Tel Aviv, and conveniently located near the north-south highway I would be taking. Lod, I read, was once an Arab city called Lydda. During the 1948 Arab-Israeli War, Israel invaded Lydda and expelled most of the Arabs, then renamed the city Lod and populated it with Jewish immigrants. Where had the former Arab inhabitants of Lydda gone? From Lod, my drive would take me south, directly between Gaza and the West Bank (apparently there was no way to avoid squeezing through those two volatile areas!) and on to Be'er Sheva. From Be'er Sheva, I would head east on the east-west highway that led to Arad.

I knew from previous family trips that I would have to travel light to keep up with Mark, who had just a single backpack. In my small roller bag I folded a stretchy black shirt and skirt that I could wear every day, sleep in every night, and wash and hang dry when necessary. I added a few extra shirts, a vaguely Palestinian-looking scarf, and a bathing suit for the Dead Sea. In my extra-large purse, I put guidebooks, maps, a box of Ticonderoga pencils, my red hardback Moleskine journal, camera, laptop, and new cell phone.

On Tuesday morning, June 23, just before I left our home for the airport, Mark called using Skype. His phone, though no longer working for voice service, could still receive text messages, and he suggested I text him upon my arrival at the Tel Aviv airport. He agreed with me about driving in the West Bank—no car there. His *Let's Go* itinerary had him traveling by bus or service taxi (an inexpensive shared taxi) in Israel and the West Bank, except for three days in the Dead Sea area, where he was supposed to rent a cheap stick shift. So, in the West Bank at least, we'd take buses or service taxis. Mark said he'd met an American professor who had been to the West Bank, and she'd cautioned him that anything we took through the checkpoint between Israel and the West Bank could be inspected and confiscated by the Israeli military. As we talked, I jettisoned the camera and laptop. "Good luck, Mom," Mark said.

What is Hebrew for "Women's Restroom"?

Tuesday, June 23.

Armed guards at the departure gate at Newark International Airport for the flight to Tel Aviv blocked me and other passengers from entering the seating area at the gate until thirty minutes before departure time "for security reasons." Was there an emergency? I slipped my iPhone out of my bag and looked for "airport incidents on Israeli flights." Pages of entries appeared, but no recent incidents. Apparently, Israeli flights are allowed to depart only from airports (or airport areas) that follow the strict Israeli security guidelines. Israeli transportation officials often train airport guards throughout the world. I took a seat at a nearby gate and began checking out the other waiting passengers, hoping to find someone also on the flight to Tel Aviv, someone I could talk to about Israel. A cluster of bearded men in dark suits and hats and long side curls in front of their ears stood in a protective semicircle around an equal number of women in ankle-length skirts with shirt collars buttoned at the neck, shirt sleeves concealing their arms, and loosely crocheted nets covering their hair. Each woman held a newborn child in her arms. I assumed that these families were Israeli. Was it common for Israeli women to travel to the United States to give birth? What denomination or sect of Judaism did they belong to?

Suddenly, I regretted my ignorance of Jewish religion and customs, but as I had a three-hour layover in Newark, I had time to begin some reading. I dug through my purse for a guidebook. In the section on religion, I learned that ultra-Orthodox Jewish men, like the extremely conservative Haredim, wear black coats and hats and have beards and side curls, called *peyot*. The women dress modestly and cover most exposed hair and skin. I glanced back up at the couples. With my iPhone, I searched the Internet for "peyot" and discovered the tradition stems from a biblical interpretation that condemns shaving the "corners" of the head. In some sects of Orthodox Judaism, peyot are long, neat, and dangling in front of their ears, like those of the men who stood near me, but in other sects, peyot are tightly twisted in protruding coils or wrapped several times around the ears. How could I have lived so long without learning about things like peyot?

A middle-aged woman with short, orange-red hair and a flowered, knee-length dress sank into the seat directly across from me. She rummaged through one of her many shopping bags, retrieving nothing, and then began to tug at her hem in a vain attempt to cover her knees, which were held apart by ample thighs. I waited until she was done and then asked whether she was waiting for the flight to Tel Aviv. "Russian," she said. Perhaps I had not adequately framed my question. I asked again, and her response was the same, "Russian." We just sat there looking at each other and smiling, and then she elaborated, "Russian. Be'er Sheva," and that was the end of our conversation.

Once again, I pulled out my iPhone and typed in "Russians in Israel." During the 1990s, there had been a large influx of Russian Jews into Israel, and today, with nearly one million Russian immigrants in the country, Russian is the most widely spoken nonofficial language in Israel. The mass immigration from Russia and other countries like Ethiopia, Morocco, India, Syria, Iraq, France, and the United States was a result of Israel's "law of return," which grants Israeli citizenship to anyone who is a Jew or a child or grandchild of a Jew, and also to anyone who is the spouse of a Jew, or the spouse of a child or grandchild of a Jew. I never realized how simple it was for any Jew in the world, or person related to a Jew, to obtain full Israeli citizenship.

I sat fully intent upon my Internet research until about thirty minutes before departure when a security guard opened the gate to the seating area for the flight to Tel Aviv. After uniformed agents re-screened each passenger and carefully inspected each piece of carry-on luggage, we filed through the boarding tunnel onto the plane. My preassigned seat was next to a young man in a black suit and black hat. He wore his hair short with no side curls. My preflight research indicated that he was probably Orthodox but not ultra-Orthodox. He told me that he lived and worked in New York and he was going to Israel for his wedding. His fiancée had taken an earlier flight and was waiting for him in Tel Aviv, where her family was making the wedding preparations. I told my seatmate that I was going to Israel to visit my son who was working on a writing assignment. I omitted the part about rescuing Mark from terrorists. The young man asked no questions.

With most passengers settled in their seats and the flight attendants making their pre-departure rounds, I quickly took this last opportunity to check my phone messages. (I had not purchased international service with AT&T, and for the duration of the trip, I'd be communicating by text messages or email—or if need be, by very expensive phone calls.) There were two messages in my in-box. The first was from my mother in Florida. While watching her morning exercise program, she had seen a news alert flash across the television screen announcing a large-magnitude earthquake somewhere in Alaska. *How large?* She hoped Rex and Paul were okay. She did not mention my rescue mission to the Middle East. The second message, which I listened to just as the flight attendant announced that passengers must turn off all electronic devices, was from my friend Sandra in Houston. Her voice was tense. Widespread fighting was breaking out between Hamas and Fatah in the West Bank. "If you're not on the plane yet, don't get on!"

I slipped my phone back into my purse and turned to my young seatmate. Had he heard anything about the Alaska earthquake? Widespread fighting between Palestinian factions in the West Bank? He said, politely, he had not. Then he opened the book on his lap and read until his head lolled to one side and his soft, *pfuffing* sounds signaled sleep.

For a brief moment, his regular breathing became the soundtrack to my slippery grasp on hope . . . hope that the earthquake was far from Skagway and the Chilkoot Trail, hope that the fighting in the West Bank was nowhere near the highway that, in just a few hours, would take me to Mark. I saw myself behind the wheel of a nondescript rental car, wrestling with maps on my dashboard as I drove along the road between the West Bank and Gaza, dodging bullets on one side and rockets on the other. My thoughts tilted heavily toward the fearful end of the conjecture scale. What if were struck by a Hamas rocket? How could I rescue my son if I were blown up? And, while not on the level of my other life-or-death concerns, I had some very real, practical considerations to address. What if I had to stop along the way to use a restroom? Would I even recognize a gas station? Were the restrooms clearly marked for women? What was Hebrew for "women's restroom"? Russian? I knew there were some things I couldn't control, but there were some that I could—I would forego any beverages for the last half of the twelve-hour flight so I wouldn't have to stop at a restroom.

Wednesday, June 24.

At nine o'clock in the morning, the flight attendant announced our impending arrival at Ben Gurion International Airport, and I watched as the clouds parted and the high-rise hotels and condos of Tel Aviv rose over the silver-blue Mediterranean that edged our horizon. We descended onto tarmac cut through the coastal plains of central Israel, flat and brown with patches of low, green shrubs, a stark contrast to the tall, glistening outline of Tel Aviv to the northeast.

I texted Mark, "I just arrived!" A few minutes later, Mark texted back, "Great! Meet me at the tourist office in Arad at noon."

As I made my way through the airport, I understood what Mark had said about Israel being a "cosmopolitan" place. The glass-enclosed terminal passageway for arriving international passengers overlooked a contemporary rotunda with a Segafredo Espresso, McDonald's, numerous ATMs, a synagogue, duty-free stores advertising diamonds and gold, and several sleek newsstands where short-skirted women browsed through *Vogue* magazines from four continents. I wondered whether I should have packed something more exciting than my black stretchy skirt and top, but the wardrobe die was cast, and besides, my bag was completely full.

The passageway led to a glass-enclosed people-mover called "the connector," which transported international passengers to passport control. The young, female deputy at passport control stared into my eyes, closely examined my passport, and questioned me repeatedly about my birthplace, Libya, and the purpose of my trip to Israel. Having been raised in an air force family and being married to a litigator, I remained unfazed. She paused momentarily, gauging my breathing rate. Then, very abruptly, she smiled and waved me through. Nearby, I exchanged dollars for shekels and then quickly located the car rental area. And I was in luck; there was a business just steps away called "GPS4RENT." The agent was kind enough to program the navigation device for me and set the tourist office in Arad as my destination. (Yes, Chaim, these people are helpful!)

Few cars were on the stark strip of blacktop leading south to the Negev Desert. The sky was clear and blue, the air hot and dry. Terraced groves, low hills dotted with trees, and wheat-colored grasses of the coastal plains gradually gave way to brown mounds of rock and dust. The young Israeli rental agent who had programmed my navigation device said it was possible for a rocket launched from Gaza to hit the highway. "I'm setting this thing so you won't see any Arabs," he added with a smile. But this was no joke. My fingers ached from the tight grip I had on the steering wheel. What if I can't find Mark? What if I get lost? What if I'm abducted by Hamas militants? I glanced east toward the West Bank, but saw no signs of fighting, and then west toward Gaza, scanning for telltale flares in the sky, but saw no rockets. More than an hour into the drive, at the northern edge of the Negev, the land was flat and strewn with jagged boulders, a desolate expanse with little sign of human habitation. The scorching desert air seeped into the compact car. The air conditioner slowly stopped cooling. I felt my contact lenses crinkling in my eyes. I was parched.

Near Arad, the navigation device, in its clipped British accent, directed me through a maze of neatly landscaped traffic roundabouts to the tourist office, where I was to meet Mark. The view was fuzzy. Wavy lines distorted the scenery. Dashboard controls were difficult to interpret. I pulled over, careful not to turn off the car for fear that it would deactivate the navigation device, and texted Mark: "I'm at the tourist office!" Several minutes passed. The sun cut mercilessly through the windshield. I thought about how sad it would be if I died of dehydration before seeing my son. My phone beeped, alerting me to a text from him: "Are you at the tourist office in town or the one outside of town?" Unbelievable! Two tourist offices in this tiny desert town? I needed water or I was going to pass out. I couldn't risk spending even a second to text Mark back. I slammed my foot on the gas and sped wildly through a few more roundabouts. I spotted a market tucked in a courtyard off the street. I pulled the car over, turned the ignition off (navigation device be damned!), ran into the market, and bought two bottles of water. Back in the car, I sat drinking the ice-cold water. There was a knock on the passenger-side window. I looked up. It was Mark.

The Future Population of Arad is Fifty Thousand

Wednesday, June 24, noon.

Mark's smiling face pressed against the front passenger window. My hands gripped the steering wheel, but my eyes scanned every visible inch of my son. Skin tanned by the sun. Red paisley bandana pressing back unruly, dark curls. Khaki hiking pants and white V-neck tee shirt, a little sooty and very wrinkled. Bulging olive-colored backpack over his shoulder. He opened the car door and swung his pack into the back seat, laughing at my inability to move. Together finally, in my nondescript rental car, in an obscure little desert town with a dozen neatly landscaped roundabouts, I uttered the only words I could muster: "It's Mark!"

Once Mark was inside the car, I held onto him with both hands, and question tumbled over question. He seemed just as excited to see me, and our questions and answers overlapped to such an extent that any onlooker would have had a very hard time deciphering our tangled code. But all was clear to me. Mark was safe. He was happy. He had not heard the recent news about Fatah and Hamas fighting in the West Bank or the high-intensity quake in Alaska, and he wasn't particularly concerned about either. The males in our household are all disturbingly calm in the face of catastrophe. Rex and Paul would not huddle by the campfire time-tracking my every movement on this journey, nor would they assume I was tensely waiting to hear from them as I followed news of the earthquake. Mark was cut from the same cloth. I would try to follow his lead and live in this delicious, present moment.

We sat in the car catching up on the details of our past two days' trials and adventures until we both realized we were hungry. In fact, Mark was famished. The previous day he'd eaten only peanut butter and the stale pita bread stashed in his backpack. We would remain in Arad just long enough to have lunch and for Mark to inspect some hotel rooms for *Let's Go*.

Mark said there were two good restaurants in Arad. There were dozens of small food vendors tucked away in alleyways, and though I was willing to try them, he wanted to break me in gently to the local fare. He decided on Muza, a pub with soccer team flags ("football colours") and other sports memorabilia layering the walls and ceilings. We took a table with a clear view of the flat-screen television, which was tuned to the FIFA Confederations Cup soccer matches in South Africa. The US team would be playing top-ranked Spain in a semifinal match later that evening, and Mark wanted to keep an eye on any updates. I couldn't imagine how he managed to keep up with soccer while working in the desert.

At the table next to us, three casually dressed Israeli teens (children, really), each with an assault rifle slung over the back of his or her chair, finished off platters of burgers and fries between running soccer commentaries. I looked across the room at the dark wood-paneled bar with its ornate beer taps and rows of call liquors organized by their baroque labels. Even back in Texas, one couldn't carry weapons in a place that served alcohol. Why would anyone need assault rifles at lunch? The image simply did not line up with any experience I could call upon. Mark leaned over and whispered that the teens sitting nearby were Israeli soldiers and required to carry their weapons even when off-duty. Israeli high-school graduates are required to serve in the Israeli forces, boys for three years, girls for two years. "There are Israeli soldiers all over the Negev," he said, reminding me of his trip to Mitzpe Ramon with a bus full of new Israeli Defense Forces recruits. "I talked to a soldier riding next to me about his rifle, thinking how cool it'd be to be in the military, and he told me he'd rather be free to travel like me."

While Mark reviewed the menu, I pulled out my iPhone and quickly scanned the latest news. I found no mention of fighting in the West Bank, but there was a brief report about the earthquake in Alaska: a magnitude 5.4 earthquake had struck near Anchorage. Anchorage was hundreds of miles from the Chilkoot Trail. Satisfied that Mark and I were not subject to imminent attack and that Rex and Paul were probably out of harm's way, a waterfall of tension, built up during my long flight over the Atlantic, poured out of my neck and shoulders.

Then we came to the real purpose of this particular stop in our journey. "I'd like the one-pound hamburger and the rib-eye steak," Mark told the somewhat astonished waitress.

Mark's conversation overflowed with anecdotes from his travels, most involving food. "In Petra, half a roast chicken with rice and cardamom costs six dollars, probably because it's such a tourist trap. But you could get street food for fifty cents, and I ate the best falafel I've ever had from a roadside stand there. Turned out," he added, "there was a hidden price to pay. Several times a day for a whole week afterwards I'd have to run into a store or restaurant and say something like, 'I'll have a vanilla ice cream—and, by the way, where's your bathroom?' And, there is the really cheap sushi in the Negev," he continued. "Because the desert is only a hundred fifty meters above sea level, there's brackish water just under the desert surface. It's apparently a big business pumping the water into tanks where they farm fish. You know how I love sushi, so I was real excited about finally being able to afford something other than peanut butter and questionable street offerings. So I ordered tuna sushi for lunch one day, only to find out too late that tuna is the one fish they don't farm in the Negev. My stomach churned all afternoon. I think I am permanently scarred in the sushi department."

Watching Mark laugh and tell stories about his gastrointestinal disasters lifted all my worries and freed me to laugh until we were both in stitches. The world felt right again for the first time in weeks. This was the boy I remembered, the little boy who adored hamburgers and barbecue, the college freshman who asked us to please send him an entire five-pound brisket from The Salt Lick so he could share it with his dorm-mates, all East Coast natives. Mark's driven hunger was my final and absolute proof that he was alive, intact, and in perfect working order. I swear I could not stop laughing. From time to time, the young Israeli soldiers glanced back at us over their rifles, amused.

In between bites of his one-pound burger, Mark quizzed our waitress about the restaurant and jotted notes in a purple pocket-sized notebook, the front of which he had neatly labeled with the word "ARAD." In the Negev, he said, he had been focusing less on restaurant fare and more on "hard facts," such as the hours and location of grocery stores, hostels, and other budget-friendly places, because so many backpackers and campers frequent the Negev. Arad, though, is on the northeastern edge of the Negev, and travelers stopping in the city may be heading east to the Dead Sea resorts. In that case, they probably have enough money to eat at a restaurant like Muza. So Mark would be reviewing his one-pound hamburger and rib-eye steak, no doubt in glowing terms, for *Let's Go*. I watched as he asked questions and took notes.

In another corner, a table of six young men and women were speaking what we thought was surely Russian. I told Mark what I had read about the Russian immigration into Israel. Then he told me something I'd not read. "People come here from all over because Israel offers them subsidized housing—some don't even consider themselves Jewish." Mark reached in his backpack for the brochure about Arad that he had picked up at the tourist office. "It's all about getting people to settle the land, and Israel lures immigrants with cheap housing and economic incentives like tax breaks," he said, pointing to the glossy, four-color wonder. "Says here that Arad's current population is twenty-seven thousand and its future population is fifty thousand—and that residents get a thirteen percent discount on income tax." Mark suspected that Israel's incentives to settle the land coincided with the nation's political motives. "Israel," he said, "wants to settle the Negev with non-Arab voters who will support the state of Israel."

As Mark spoke, I listened, taken by his interest in the subtleties of Israeli politics and culture. Back home he had taken apart computers, climbed any surface with a significant incline and dangerous altitude, and excelled in school. He had worked on political campaigns of family friends, and we spent many family dinners debating national political issues. But here, he had an entirely new focus.

After cleaning every bite from his plate, Mark sketched out a review of his meal: "Excellent" he wrote in his ARAD notebook.

Mark wanted to complete his review of the nearby Hotel Inbar, a modern, multistory, concrete-and-glass edifice with an indoor swimming pool and spa. He asked me to stay in the car. His modus operandi had been to tell hotel clerks that his family was coming to town and he wanted to see a few rooms. That story wouldn't work with his mother in tow. In a rare moment of detachment, I realized I was not, even after all the drama of the past weeks, staging a rescue. In that brief moment of stillness, I also realized I was exhausted from the long trip. I had made a conscious decision not to interfere with Mark's work while we traveled together, and I was more than content to wait in the car and browse the literature he had gathered about Arad. One tourist brochure described the city as having especially clean air. *"Magic in the air!"* it proclaimed on its cover. The brochure said the site for the city (a plateau six hundred meters above sea level) was selected because of its proximity to the Dead Sea, the views, and the climate. It was ninety degrees, at least, the sun still beating down, though not at all humid. I detected a slight breeze. Magic? Finding Mark certainly felt magical. I would have to acclimate myself a little more in order to pass judgment on the air.

Mark returned after inspecting the hotel rooms, raving about the plush mattresses, so much softer than a yoga mat on a concrete floor. We consulted the road map, and Mark programmed the navigation device. It did not occur to me to program the device, as the Israeli rental agent at the airport claimed to have done, so we "wouldn't see any Arabs."

Welcome to the Lowest Spot on Earth

Wednesday, June 24, afternoon.

Our destination was the guesthouse at Ein Gedi Kibbutz, which is set on a plateau bordering the western bank of the Dead Sea. We drove southwest from Arad along a perfectly smooth blacktopped road winding through the sandstone hills of the northern Negev Desert to the Dead Sea, which is the lowest spot on earth. I leaned back in my seat and allowed myself to be taken in by the cloudless blue sky, the endless beige and peach rolling hills, and the absence of any green living thing. There was not a single tree for miles and miles. Glancing out the passenger window, Mark remarked that the hills were perfect for mountain biking. He scribbled a few hasty lines in the notebook he'd left out on the dashboard. I tried to envision Mark hurdling bike and body over the dunes with stray bullets and homemade projectiles kicking up sprays of sand all around him. Then I tried not to. I had not yet turned off my protective, mothering switch.

A half hour into our drive, a layer of salty haze settled below the sky, and we could see the aquamarine waters of the Dead Sea. We turned north on a road that paralleled the banks of the sea, pulling off to the shoulder shortly afterward to stare in wide-eyed awe at salt-encrusted pockets of electric blue water that sparkled like gemstones and mottled the sand between road and sea. Mark speculated the crystalline formations had developed as the salty water from the Dead Sea (which actually is a lake, not a sea) evaporated. Whatever the "science" behind the phenomenon, this was full-on beauty.

Twenty-five miles or so north along the road paralleling the Dead Sea, a sign directed us up the rocky incline of a long, narrow plateau to Ein Gedi Kibbutz. Midway up the plateau, the barren earth transformed into a fertile mass of hedged shrubs and flowering plants. A guard confirmed our reservation, opened the automatic gate blocking the road, and waved us through. As we rounded the final curve to the top of the plateau, the air passing through the botanical gardens filled our car with sweet, indefinable floral scents. A circular drive around a cactus garden led to the guest reception area, a low, one-story building with a gift shop, a synagogue, and a café-bar facing both inside toward the lobby and outside to a decked patio overlooking the Dead Sea. The glass doors of the guest reception area opened to a sprawling lawn shaded by huge trees and circled by a path, which diverged like spokes in a wheel throughout the gardens to the guest rooms.

We found my room tucked in a grove of palms and oleanders on the northern edge of the kibbutz. Green spiked fronds and pink desert roses framed the entryway. There was a tiny patio furnished with two lawn chairs and a retractable clothesline. Inside were a set of twin beds, a small dresser, and a desk with a basket of ripe apples, figs, and dates. Chaim had said the accommodations were "sparse, but totally acceptable," and the kibbutz website had described the rooms as "rustically elegant and very comfortable." The room was all of those things. Though the original plan was for me to stay at the kibbutz and Mark at a youth hostel nearby, he made a quick decision, influenced to a great degree by the basket of fruit, the extra bed, and the proximity to the café-bar, to stay with me at the kibbutz.

Mark poured out the entire contents of his backpack onto one of the narrow beds. The items revealed the story of his professional life as a travel writer in this harsh land: wooden matches and a stove fashioned from a tin can; a jar of peanut butter and the crusty remains of stale pita bread; crimson-colored packets of Turkish coffee; a titanium cup; a small first-aid kit wrapped in duct tape; a hefty tube of Egyptian shaving cream and a disposable razor; brochures about scuba diving adventures in the Gulf of Aqaba; leaflets about sunset camel tours, horseback riding trips, and traditional Bedouin-style dinners; an Israeli hostel guide and national bus schedule and other note-filled pamphlets; multiple pocket-sized notebooks on which Mark had written "Petra," "Eilat," "Nuweiba," "Be'er Sheva," and "Arad"; a few tattered and dog-eared novels and guidebooks; a small package bound in plastic, which Mark told me was a gift for his girlfriend, Beryl (whom I imagined might be enjoying a frutti di bosco gelato at the Piazza della Signoria); a pair of threadbare orange and blue flowered board shorts and two well-worn tee shirts; and a pair of hiking boots and dirty wool socks that actually *crunched* as they fell out of the pack. As Mark described the significance of various items, I felt like an archaeologist analyzing a culture from relics heretofore alien to me.

While Mark showered away days of desert and campfire smoke, I looked over a brochure I found on the desk about the kibbutz's botanical gardens. On the cover was a biblical reference to Ein Gedi: *"My beloved is to me a cluster of henna blossoms, from the vineyards of Ein Gedi* (Song of Solomon, 1:14)." The brochure said Ein Gedi was once a fertile area known for its perfume gardens and vineyards, but the gardens and vineyards disappeared sometime after the Byzantine era. When the kibbutz was established in 1959, its founders reclaimed the land by planting specimens from all parts of the world, and now the kibbutz's gardens included more than a thousand different plants from five continents. Date, fig, olive, and pomegranate trees shaded small groves and walkways. Over forty species of palm arched over doorways and well-tended gardens. The brochure detailed the origins of many kibbutz plants—like the African myrrh, which it described as a sturdy gray-green bush with an aromatic resin used for incense, cosmetics, and perfume, brought to the kibbutz "from the deserts of Ethiopia by Prof. Yehuda Felix, and successfully acclimatized." Though many of the imports were drought-resistant and suitable for Ein Gedi's desert climate, other specimens were tropical and better suited to a Central American rainforest. To sustain this improbable mesh of biodiversity, a vast irrigation system diverted water from the natural springs that supplied the kibbutz with fresh water and showered it on acres of gardens. But more than fifty years of development in the Dead Sea area had propelled the region into a water crisis, the brochure reported, and the ecologically conscious kibbutz members were making an effort to transition to more native, drought-hardy species, hence the cactus garden.

After Mark showered and dressed in his only clean shirt and shorts, we strolled on a series of linking paths through the garden toward the café-bar. There, on the eastern edge of the plateau, we sat at a tree-shaded picnic table with a magnificent view of the blue waters of the Dead Sea and, in the distance beyond, the brown ridges of Jordan's Edom Mountains. A waiter about Mark's age, named Zamir, brought us two frosted mugs of Goldstar, Israel's ubiquitous domestic beer. Zamir had an engaging smile, and like most young Israelis, spoke perfect English. His unmasked curiosity about us made him appear younger than he was, innocent. Mark told Zamir we were tourists, but said nothing about his affiliation with *Let's Go.* He never revealed he was writing a guidebook before completing his review of an establishment. If the sight of a mother and adult son together on vacation seemed odd to Zamir, he revealed no surprise. Zamir told us he was working at the kibbutz as part of a "preferred jobs program" for Israeli soldiers who had completed their compulsory military service. His job at the kibbutz would last three months and after that maybe he would go on to a university. The public universities in Israel were some of the best in the world, he said, and the government subsidized tuition for Israeli students. Zamir was uncertain about what he would do if he didn't go on to school, but thought perhaps he'd travel.

As sunset approached, Mark and I walked through the gardens from the café-bar to the main guest restaurant, surreptitiously crushing leaves of shrubbery we passed and inhaling their exotic scents in our cupped hands. Along the way, we passed a school building with a playground, a reminder that the kibbutz was not just a resort but also home to hundreds of permanent residents. It was a self-sustaining community with housing units and a theater, a clinic, a grocery store, and a cemetery. Nearing the restaurant, the path took us through a pocket park along the southwestern edge of the plateau, which dropped into a cavernous *wadi* (a dry valley that becomes a watercourse during the rainy season) called Nahal Arugot. Where we stood in the park, the soft grasses, flowering shrubs, and tropical plants were extravagant and luxurious in their greens, fuchsias, and golds. But from our vantage point at the brink of the plateau, as far as we could see beyond lay a desert of sand and rocky cliffs in shades of muted yellows and tans.

A short, solid woman greeted us at the door of the guest restaurant. The red hibiscus embedded in her curly hair did little to soften her brusque, military manner, perhaps acquired during her days of compulsory service in the Israeli military. Mark was instantly hypnotized by the buffet, with its offerings of whole fried tilapia, chicken schnitzel, salads with ripe tomatoes and cucumbers and couscous, hummus with olive oil and pine nuts, and both chocolate and vanilla cakes. Mark piled his plate with food. While we ate and talked, young men and women in white shirts and black pants, probably also working here as part of the Israeli military's "preferred jobs" program, set out food, cleared dishes, and poured coffee. Mark's conversation was less about food and more about the future. "I'm meeting Beryl in

Paris when I finish my job with *Let's Go,*" he told me. "I've been reading travel blogs about how awesome Paris is, and I've made a Google map with all of the cheap cafés, Asian grocery stores, inexpensive wineries, and cinemas that play only French new wave. Paris is going to be totally awesome." He planned their adventures in Paris like an adult, yet he sounded like the boy who used to tell us how "awesome" it was to ride the Krypton Coaster at Six Flags Fiesta Texas in San Antonio. Trying not to dwell on how the word "awesome" could suffer from overuse, I relaxed into his excitement.

After dinner, Mark and I wound our way back to the room, where he gathered his computer and work materials, and then we headed for the reception area, where there were comfortable couches and wireless Internet. Mark sat and organized brochures, maps, and notes for his weekly copy batch for *Let's Go.* (A "copy batch" included a ranking of area establishments, maps, suggestions for organizing the material in the guidebook, digital photographs, handy tips, unusual "beyond tourism" opportunities, and a list of useful words and phrases to be included in the guidebook's glossary.) While Mark worked, I borrowed his laptop. There were no emails from Rex, which I took to mean, among other things, that he was not in a hospital with Internet access. That was very good news. Then searching for news about fighting in the West Bank, I discovered a report from National Public Radio. It was a transcript of a program that had played the day before, the morning I was on my connecting flight to Israel. That very morning, my friend Sandra apparently had listened to the program on the local Houston public radio station as she drove to work, and called from her cell phone to leave the message urging me to abort my trip. "Fatah leaders say Hamas is plotting to take over the West Bank by force, in a move similar to the events of 2007 when Hamas fighters overwhelmed Fatah forces and took control of the Gaza Strip," NPR reported. "Over the past few weeks, Palestinian Authority security forces have fought two gun battles with Hamas militants. I checked the map. We were sitting less than a mile from the West Bank. That was very, very *bad* news.

A Bedouin Disneyland

Thursday, June 25.

I awoke feeling as though I'd lived an entire week during the previous twenty-four hours. Though it may have been true that some part of me had secretly come for the adventure, I had hoped to space out the excitement a little more evenly. Today I would accompany Mark, maintaining a discreet distance while he worked, to the Israeli national monument Masada, the upscale beach resort Ein Bokek, and the "Bedouin camp" Kfar Hanokdim. In the evening, we planned to take a long, circuitous drive through the Judean hills to the western entrance of Masada for a sound and light show. I took one last luxurious stretch before reaching for my map of Israel on the table by my bed. Our itinerary, I noted with relief, would lead us south of Ein Gedi Kibbutz, relatively removed from whatever trouble was brewing between Fatah and Hamas in the West Bank. I had a day to be a tourist, to reconnect with my son with no rescues or emergencies on my agenda.

A few minutes later, Mark was awake and splashing the kibbutz's fresh springwater on his face in our small bathroom. As I assembled the things I would need for a full day of touring, Mark collected the items required for his *Let's Go* research and then took a few minutes to wash his crunchy hiking socks and clip them to the clothesline before we departed for Masada.

Masada, set on a plateau south of Ein Gedi, is an archaeological site bearing the remains of a once-palatial stone fortress that served as a refuge for Jewish zealots from their Roman oppressors during the First Jewish-Roman War. According to the story, Roman General Cornelius Flavius Silva commanded a siege of the fortress with a legion of eight thousand men. Inside the palace, nine hundred Jewish fighters (we later learned that they were somewhat radical Sicarii, a Jewish sect antagonistic to both other Jews and Romans) defended the fortress until it was clear they would not survive the Roman onslaught. Rather than live in shame as Roman slaves, they systematically killed one another, with the last living man killing himself, so they would leave the world as free men. When the Romans arrived, they discovered only a few surviving members of the Jewish sect—two women and five children—who were spared in order to keep the memory of the martyrs alive. The story of Masada has become a metaphor for the continuing struggle to defend Israel, and Masada has become a Jewish cultural icon. It is the place where Israeli Defense Forces recruits take their military oath ("Masada shall not fall again"), and a sight that even Chaim had said we should not miss.

After fifteen minutes of driving, Mark and I reached the monument and boarded the cable car that transports visitors to the top of the plateau, where we explored the ruins at a pace slowed by the almost unbearable heat. We stopped at one particularly scenic (and shaded) spot to take pictures. Another refugee from the incessant sun and heat edged his way into our crowded little patch of shade. Gil was from California, and his last trip to Masada was nearly thirty years ago when his father worked on the set of *Masada*, a movie starring Peter O'Toole. Forgoing the cable-car option, Gil had just hiked up the Roman Ramp, a steep path up the western side of the plateau. He stood in his perspiration-soaked shirt gulping water from an icy bottle bought from a refreshment stand set among the ruins, and he described some of his memories. Gil's father was a caterer to the stars, a man whose culinary services were sought by producers of Hollywood movies filmed in Israel. He served the casts and crews of *Remembrance of Love* (1982), *A Woman Called Golda* (1982), *Triumph of the Spirit* (1989), and *The Finest Hour* (1991), among others. During the filming of *A Woman Called Golda*, Ingrid Bergman was suffering from cancer. Gil's father cooked special meals for her, and they became friends. Of all the movies, *Masada* was one of the most challenging to cater. It was long before bodies could be digitally created, and the army scenes required a battalion of soldiers. There were hundreds of people on the set, living in tents for the duration of the production and eating three meals a day. At the conclusion of the filming of *Masada*, Gil's father was presented with a gift: a full set of armor worn by one of the Roman soldiers, which included a realistic-looking heavy metal crest, shield, and cuirass. A little "starstruck," Mark compared notes with Gil on historic facts and several Hollywood notables. They talked about the pyrotechnic light show later in the evening that highlighted the story of the siege.

Decidedly less dramatic than Masada, our next stop was Ein Bokek, a touristy enclave bordering the Dead Sea, about twenty miles south of Ein Gedi Kibbutz. Ein Bokek's cluster of upscale high-rise hotels was a striking contrast to the few modest beaches, hostels, and kibbutzim that dotted the rest of the Dead Sea coast. At the resort's gated entrance, an Israeli guard motioned us to a stop, checked our passports, and inspected the inside of the car and trunk. After Mark explained he was writing for a travel guide, the guard opened the gate and allowed us to enter. Mark parked the car in front of a modest one-story strip mall and set out on foot with the sun reflecting off the towering hotels and concrete walkways, even glinting off his black hair.

I was accustomed to the heat in Texas, but this was considerably hotter than the warmest summer day back home. As Mark disappeared around the end of the shopping center, I hurried inside the air-conditioned mall and wandered through a succession of shops selling Dead Sea health and beauty products. There were rows and rows of aromatic compounds created from the salt and mud dredged from the sea: mineral mud masks, sea-salt body scrubs and foot soaks, oil-infused black mud, and more. Though located next to a famous tourist attraction and offering an array of affordable, yet luxurious, products, there were few shoppers in the stores. "There used to be more tourists here," a salesclerk explained, "but the international news is so pro-Palestinian these days that it keeps people from coming." I was taken aback by her comment. In the United States, it seemed to me, we heard very little good news about the Palestinians. Even as I stood there listening to her, the words "Palestinian," "terrorist," and "suicide bomber" raced through my mind and were so intertwined that I couldn't pull them apart. Looking back at the shelves of beauty products, I realized I had no room in my one small carry-on suit-case to take a single thing home with me, but I resolved to visit the kiosk that sold Dead Sea products at the Barton Creek Mall back in Austin and buy that cream the young Israeli salesclerks insist will banish the dark circles and wrinkles under my eyes.

After window-shopping, I waited for Mark at Aroma, a cof-fee shop in the mall that was so close to the McDonald's next door that I could read the menu. I noticed there were no cheese-burgers among the menu items. Apparently, even Israelis who do not strictly follow a kosher diet find the meat-cheese combina-tion distasteful. Although I was vegetarian and had not tasted a cheeseburger for years, the smell of burgers and fries reminded me how much I once loved those greasy, salty morsels. When I was eight months pregnant with Mark, I drove through a McDonald's on my way home from work one night and ordered two Quar-ter Pounder (with cheese) *meals*, both of which I consumed while driving home to have dinner with Rex.

In addition to lattes rivaling Starbucks, Aroma had free wire-less. I pulled out my iPhone. Among the numerous emails from my mother and sisters inquiring about my whereabouts and safety were two from Rex. He and Paul had hiked the Chilkoot Trail, and this was his full report: "We made it! Fantastic trip. Just back. Tired and sore and taking our guide to dinner." His sec-ond email contained only a photograph, taken from the window of the tiny "Wings of Alaska" plane somewhere between Juneau and Skagway, and it made my heart sink. Framed by an airplane wing on the upper left and a frightfully close mountain range on the lower right, and blurred by a foggy mist, it pictured gray and black cumulus clouds billowing over snowcapped mountains. But I was relieved. I knew Rex and Paul were safe. They had survived the hike. And they had survived what appeared to have been a daredevil flight.

Mark arrived at Aroma with stacks of brochures, pamphlets, and menus. He ordered a latte, and out of habit, I paid. We were still in the "in between" stage of our relationship. He told me he wouldn't include much of the information he'd collected in his *Let's Go* copy batch because most of Ein Bokek's hotels and restaurants were too expensive for the guidebook's readers, but he had discovered a few affordable eateries. "There's a mini-mart near the beach that makes delicious *shwarma*, and it's cheap!" Not far from the mini-mart was a car rental agency (the only one in the entire Dead Sea area), and Mark had stopped by to check on renting a car for his work with *Let's Go*. After noting the exorbitant prices, he decided against getting his own car. "It's a waste of money for *Let's Go* when I can just borrow yours—I can borrow yours, can't I?" Yes, we were still "in between."

While making his rounds at Ein Bokek, Mark had made another interesting discovery. When the resort was first built, its beaches bordered the waters of the southern basin of the Dead Sea. Since that time, the southern basin had completely dried up due to overuse of the waters that feed the sea. The Jordan River fed fresh water into the Dead Sea, but the major springs and tributaries that flowed into the Jordan had all been dammed or diverted for drinking or irrigation. This reduced the fresh water flowing into the Dead Sea so much that it was not enough to offset the evaporation rate in the sea's shallower southern basin. When the southern basin dried up, a chemical company called Dead Sea Works began pumping water from the northern basin into the southern basin and using the southern area as evaporation ponds for extracting chemicals, mainly potash for fertilizer. Mark pulled out his map of Israel and pointed to the two blue basins of the Dead Sea separated by a thin strip of land called the Lisan Peninsula. I slipped on my reading glasses. Looking closely at the southern basin, I discovered there was no reference to the Dead Sea at all—the area was labeled "Salt Ponds." It was ironic, and sad, that guests of the ritziest Dead Sea hotels were floating in evaporation ponds used for potash production.

I mentioned the comment made by the Israeli clerk about the international news being pro-Palestinian. Mark relayed similar comments he'd heard from several Israelis in connection with the speech President Obama made in Cairo two weeks before. One stumbling block in the Israeli-Palestinian peace negotiations was Israel's continuing policy of building Israeli housing areas, called "settlements," in the West Bank—part of the territory designated by the UN to be part of the future Arab (Palestinian) state. In his speech in Cairo, Obama called for Israel to stop building settlements in the West Bank. "Israelis think Obama is more interested in Palestinian statehood than he is in Israel's security, and Palestinians think Obama isn't pushing hard enough for a Palestinian state." As Mark recounted what he'd learned in his short time working in Egypt and Israel, I thought about the salesclerk's comment about the international news being pro-Palestinian. I didn't necessarily agree with her—I had just come from an environment where I believed the media painted Palestinians largely as terrorists—but at least I better understood the basis for her remark.

From Ein Bokek, we drove through the hills toward Arad and then north to the Kfar Hanokdim Bedouin camp. By now, of course, the mere word "Bedouin" roused a whole slew of associations for me and I was very curious about this next attraction. The place was advertised as an authentic Bedouin oasis where visitors could enjoy Bedouin hospitality, learn about Bedouin life and culture, and enjoy "all kosher" Bedouin meals. There, sitting between picture-postcard palms, stood huge Bedouin-style tents and a Bedouin marketplace with rows of stalls, similar to those you'd see at a carnival, selling Bedouin teas, treats, and tourist trinkets. A giant canopy shaded a fire over which a man in full desert robes was preparing a traditional Bedouin feast. A boy wearing a long white shirt over trousers, similar to the clothing Mark described from Salah's beach camp, wandered through the tourists smiling broadly as he announced guided camel and donkey rides. Mark conferred with the staff and then ducked into the huge sleeping tent, which was furnished with colorful Oriental carpets and cushions, and recorded his findings in one of his pocket-sized notebooks. Meanwhile, I stood alone outside the main tent and watched as a group of laughing, jostling teens boarded a bus bound for the Masada sound and light show. As the light faded, the camels stirring in a nearby corral were silhouetted against twilight, and the melody of a Bedouin harp and the aroma of barbecuing lamb kabobs floated over me in the stillness of the evening. For a brief moment, I felt some of the childlike fascination I'd experienced growing up in Libya for these mysterious desert people and their way of life.

The lamb kabobs, however alluring, were not on our menu. Once again back in the car and on our way to the sound and light show, Mark seemed a little edgy, irritated by the display at Kfar Hanokdim, which he referred to as a "Bedouin Disneyland." Most of the Bedouins he had seen while working in the Negev lived in slums and certainly none in luxurious tent camps like Kfar Hanokdim. The Bedouin had herded in the Negev for centuries before Israel was created. Since then, however, the Israeli government had set aside vast tracts of land for nature reserves, military exercises, and other governmental purposes, where grazing animals were prohibited. Now, few traditional Bedouin families could make a living from herding. Mark saw some of the squalid Bedouin areas while on the bus en route to Be'er Sheva. "They carried water in buckets from water tanks and sewage flowed in ditches. They didn't even have electricity." Their reality was a far cry from the "Disneyland" we'd just visited, and Mark found the contrasts jarring. (I later read a report by the Israeli policy analysis institute Adva Center that confirmed what Mark told me: seventy-six thousand of Israel's Bedouin citizens lived in "unrecognized settlements" without electricity, sewage collection, or waste disposal, and over thirty-five thousand of those had no running water; "open rivers" of sewage from nearby Jewish towns traversed some of the settlements. Many of these settlements were near areas where Mark was working.)

The Bedouin-style display reminded Mark of Salah Mohammed's humble yet authentic Bedouin beach camp south of Nuweiba. "In the Sinai, many Bedouins, like Salah's family, have given up their traditional way of life and these days make a living from tourism, but there aren't many tourists in the Sinai now." Mark said this was apparent the minute he arrived in the area. He had taken a bus from Mt. Sinai to what was supposed to be the village of Nuweiba. The bus stop, however, was in the middle of nowhere and was on none of the maps that Mark had with him, even though they were the most current printed editions. He began walking in the direction a few cars were traveling and ended up at the Port of Nuweiba. When he arrived at the port, he was met by a uniformed Egyptian port officer, who suspected he might be Israeli. After thoroughly interrogating Mark, closely inspecting his passport, and finally accepting that Mark was American, the officer relaxed. He informed Mark that there was no longer a bus station in the village. He gave Mark walking directions along with an Arab blessing for "safe travels." When Mark arrived in the village of Nuweiba, he discovered why the bus no longer stopped there. "There was barely a reason to go there," he told me. "Ten years ago the entire area between the port and the village was looking like it was going to be a bustling tourist metropolis and everyone was developing something or other. Then tourism totally stopped because of all the news reports about terrorist attacks. Now there are half-constructed buildings up and down the coast, and the hotels that are completed are barely making it." Mark added that there was really only one hotel with people in it, which was the one he stayed in the night his wallet was stolen. When the tourists stopped coming, it must have been a huge setback for both the developers of the high-end beach hotels and the Bedouins, like Salah's family, operating humble beach camps along the coast. I began to regret my role in encouraging Mark to leave Salah's beach camp.

We spoke on and off again about the Bedouins as we continued our drive from Kfar Hanokdim to the Masada sound and light show. It was nearly dark when we reached the monument. Mark shot the car into a tiny parking spot and then set a brisk pace to the entrance. When he first told me about the Masada sound and light show, I recalled similar theatrical events we'd attended, like one Rex, Mark, Paul, and I saw at the Acropolis in Greece, where a poignant story of sacrifice deteriorated into a somewhat cheesy spectacle for tourists. I didn't share my opinion with Mark, who was looking forward to seeing the Masada show. Only a few stragglers remained outside the entrance, where we quickly bought tickets and rented headsets that would enable us to listen to the production in English. The bleachers were close to full so we made our way up to the top row. Mark and I looked around for Gil, hoping to sit near him and hear more stories about *Masada* and the other movies his father had worked on. I thought I spotted him in the front row, too far away to flag down. As we sat in the dark, the remains of the plateau fortress were illuminated in pulses of color as the narrator described in emotional detail the events surrounding the outnumbered Sicarii Jews' heroic stand against the superior Roman forces. From the first strains of the stirring musical score, the program captured Mark's attention. Following his lead, I relaxed and allowed myself to listen and watch with a (mostly) unbiased mind. It was much easier to enjoy the emotion and drama once I'd abandoned my critical analysis of the production. As a Texan, I could appreciate the Masada experience the same way I could appreciate the emotional impact of touring the Alamo. One might suspect that every "fact" was not fully accurate, yet find the whole effect emotionally potent.

When the lights in the bleachers came on and the top of the plateau disappeared into the darkness, the crowd dispersed quickly. By the time we made our way down from the top row, Gil was gone. I was not disappointed. I was tired and wanted the time on our drive back to talk. Mark seemed to have forgotten Gil altogether. As we walked to the car, Mark spoke excitedly about the highlights of the story and the production, which he found both fascinating and informative. Experiencing the evening through his unjaded perspective, I too got caught up in the moment.

Mark drove for the hour and a half or so that it took to get from the western side of Masada back to Ein Gedi Kibbutz. We talked about the Bedouin situation and how I had arrived in Israel with some preconceptions. We agreed that it was natural. Had I been wrong? I didn't know about that yet. I was still wary of travel in certain areas, still feeling protective of Mark—and myself, for that matter. Though it was near midnight when we arrived at the kibbutz, Zamir was in the lobby with a grim expression. "Michael Jackson died today," he told us. "Please come to the bar tomorrow night; I'm planning something special."

Dead Sea Perils and
Positive Energies

The sun shimmered through the pleated curtains waving softly above our beds. Mark slept soundly, the contents of his backpack strewn across the length of the tiled floor. The morning air was already warm and dry. Any dew that might have accumulated in the night was long evaporated. Mark's wool hiking socks, finally clean and soft, swayed on the patio clothesline. White butterflies circled the socks and then alighted on desert roses. The solitary sound at that hour was the cry of a bird emanating from a palm perch high above my head. Had Hamas militants launched Qassam rockets into Israel without our waking? Had they wrestled control of the West Bank from Fatah forces while Mark and I slept? I put on my new walking shoes, grabbed Mark's laptop, and walked briskly along the garden path toward the kibbutz lobby. In the distance through the gardens a couple reclined on lounge chairs under a thatched umbrella by the rippling waters of the swimming pool. Children played table tennis, and backpackers filled bottles with springwater that flowed freely from a faucet on the terrace outside the lobby. Once inside the lobby, I settled on one of the couches and opened Mark's computer. A tall, balding man with a booming voice stood at the front desk demanding to know when the shuttle bus to the kibbutz spa would arrive. On the couch opposite me, a mother fumed and scolded her preteen daughter for shaving her legs without permission. If we were about to be blown up by Hamas rockets, wouldn't that be on the top of everyone's mind? Clearly they had not read the news.

Back to the laptop, focused and determined, I hunted for news about Palestinian gun battles and Gaza rocket strikes. To my surprise and relief, there were no recent reports. So instead, I leisurely read about the Ein Gedi beach, which was on Mark's schedule for the day. That's when I came across news of something more imminent than bullets and rockets, something called "sinkholes" on the banks of the Dead Sea:

EIN GEDI, Israel—Eli Raz was peering into a narrow hole in the Dead Sea shore when the earth opened up and swallowed him. Fearing he would never be found alive, he scribbled his will on an old postcard. After 14 hours a search party pulled him from the 10-meter- (30-foot-) deep hole unhurt, and five years later the 69-year-old geologist is working to save others from a similar fate, leading an effort to map the sinkholes that are spreading on the banks of the fabled saltwater lake. These underground craters can open up in an instant, sucking in whatever lies above and leaving the surrounding area looking like an earthquake zone.

Although it had been several years since Eli Raz was sucked into the sinkhole, the MSNBC report said that just two months ago a hiker was critically injured near Ein Gedi when the ground beneath his feet suddenly opened into a thirty-foot-deep sinkhole. The article said there were about three thousand open sinkholes along the banks of the Dead Sea, and perhaps just as many more lurking beneath the surface, yet to burst open. The sinkholes began soon after Israel and Jordan began diverting the waters from the rivers and springs that fed the sea, which caused the Dead Sea waters to recede. The receding waters left newly exposed banks of sand thick with salt, and as fresh water percolated upward from underground springs, it dissolved the salt and left an unstable mass of land susceptible to sinkholes.

I looked up from the computer screen just as Mark opened the glass door and strode into the reception area. He wore a V-neck shirt and his Hawaiian-style board shorts and carried the green nylon daypack over his shoulder and a towel under his arm. When a cloud of coconut-scented sunscreen reached me, I could tell he was ready for the beach.

The Ein Gedi public beach is a mile or so north of the kibbutz. We parked the car and walked toward the water through a picnic area shaded with red umbrellas. Sections of the beach were barricaded, and signs in Hebrew and English warned of sinkholes. On the rocky shore, deeply tanned sunbathers sat on huge, salt-covered boulders and Igloo coolers, eating watermelon and drinking red soda and beer. Apart from the Martian landscape, we could have been at a picnic on any south Texas beach. A little farther down the shoreline, men with short black hair and cropped beards played backgammon under the stark sun. There were more signs posted near the beach that warned bathers not to jump, dive, splash, or drink the seawater, which was ten times saltier than the ocean, burned the eyes, and caused nausea if ingested. There was one positive effect of the thick, acrid water—bathers could float easily on the surface without the aid of flotation devices.

I happily tucked myself into the shade of one of the red umbrellas with my journal and watched as Mark waded, tentatively at first, into the saltwater and then gave himself over to the gravity-free sensation, drifting contentedly on the gentle swells. In the water near Mark, a woman in a wide-brimmed straw hat bobbed around, her body submerged except for her plump arms, dimpled knees, and a pair of red water socks with black soles. Beside her, a very pale man floated as if sitting in a chair reading a book. Another man, tanned to a leathery brown and wearing a skimpy black Speedo, stood on top of a surfboard, guiding himself with a slender oar, expertly slaloming around Mark and the other bathers who bobbed like corks on the turquoise water. Was it possible, I wondered, for a sinkhole to open up under the water, creating a giant whirlpool that would suck unsuspecting bathers "down the drain"? Could I sink into the earth any minute here on the beach? I was supposed to be relaxing so I forced myself to think of other things. I took my iPhone out and, from afar, photographed Mark enjoying this second zero-gravity float. I could picture him twenty years ago with his arms stretched out, running into the shallow waves of the Gulf of Mexico. I'm sure I envisioned

Mark as a young man many times during those days, but I never imagined the two of us together in Israel. I turned my attention away from him and used my remaining time on the beach recording the past few days in my red Moleskine journal. There was so much I wanted to remember about my trip, so many questions that remained half-formed and unanswered. Writing helped me focus my thoughts.

That night at the kibbutz restaurant, a couple from England, Tom and Susan, invited us to join them at their table. Tom, a retired professor and archaeology buff who'd spent many summers volunteering at excavations in Israel, recommended that Mark and I visit a site north of the kibbutz where we could see the unearthed remains of ancient settlements from the late Roman and Byzantine periods. There were several other dig sites in Israel, each directed by an archaeologist and affiliated with a university. A Harvard professor was managing one of those excavations at a site near Ashkelon— yes, the place that was struck last week by a Qassam rocket launched from Gaza—and had students helping with the dig. At least so far, Mark's summer job had not proved to be as hazardous as the one those budding archaeologists had signed up for!

After dinner, the four of us wandered over to the outdoor café-bar. Zamir, having prepared his tribute to Michael Jackson, continued to play the star's music all night. As we drank Goldstar and tapped our feet to "Thriller" at a picnic table on top of the plateau overlooking the Dead Sea, I thought about Chaim's comment that is a very "with it" place.

Saturday, June 27.

After breakfast at the guesthouse and with "Thriller" still playing in my head, Mark and I were on our way to "Sea of Spa," a
nearby beachside spa owned and operated by Ein Gedi Kibbutz.
White-haired tourists were streaming out of rows of tour buses
from Jerusalem when we pulled into the parking lot. Mark darted
inside the spa ahead of the deluge and quickly interviewed the
receptionist about spa offerings, hours, and so forth. The damp
air inside the spa smelled strongly of sulfur. A placard sitting on
the front desk featured a photograph of a man with a serious case
of psoriasis and advertised the benefits of soaking in the spa's
legendary indoor sulfur pools. I picked up a leaflet that extolled
the "positive energies" of Dead Sea saltwater and black mud and
described available spa services. In addition to the mundane mani-
cures, pedicures, and facials, there were sea salt massages, black
mud wraps, and sulfur water treatments, as well as reiki, watsu,
ayurveda, shiatsu, and shirodhara ("hot sesame oil poured on the
forehead to open the third eye"). The indoor sulfur pools were set
off in separate rooms. Several elderly men and women wrapped
in white towels sat on benches near the healing pools, while others, in bathing suits, soaked in the warm waters, submerged up to
their chins.

The back of the spa building opened to the sea. There, just
outside the building, Mark and I boarded a trolley to the beach.
Like the other resorts we had seen, the spa originally bordered the
beach; in those days, visitors could soak in the indoor sulfur pools
and then take a few steps outside to dip in the salty seawater. But

the Dead Sea is shrinking (mainly because of the diversion of water from the rivers that feed the sea), and now there's a mile-wide swath of land between the building and the beach. Once the trolley was filled to capacity, an aging tractor pulled it across the sand, black smoke spewing behind. It took us along a rocky path from which we could see barricades and even more signs in Hebrew and English warning visitors of sinkholes. With the trolley's slow pace, I half expected Mark to jump off and back on during our trip to the water, but he sat contained in thought, looking out over the scenery and taking the occasional note.

The trolley dropped us at a presumably safe stretch of beach where bathers floated peacefully in the thick water. The Sea of Spa brochure claimed the water contains twenty-one minerals, many found in no other sea, which "impart a relaxed feeling, nourish the skin, activate the circulatory system, and ease rheumatic and metabolic disorders." Though still partially pickled from yester-day's swim in the brine, Mark fell backward gently into the water and floated with his arms stretched out and a smile on his face, as I watched. (While I had packed a bathing suit just for this occasion, I never actually put it on, and as I stood there watching Mark, I regretted that my vanity had trumped my sharing this fun and unique experience with my son.) After his brief dip, we caught the trolley back to the spa, where tall, wooden barrels filled with the black ooze for which the Dead Sea is famous stood just outside the building. Tourists in bathing suits slathered themselves head to toe with mud, which, if truly the miracle the brochure promised, would render them perfect. Mark scooped up handfuls of the black muck and smeared it on his body and face. "It's like floating in the Dead Sea," he said. "If you come here, you just have to do it." (I didn't do it, and I didn't regret it.) He'd found an empty Gatorade bottle that he filled with mud to take with him as a gift for Beryl when he flew to Paris. It was a sweet gesture. But I wondered how he expected to get that bottle of black goo through the tight security at the Tel Aviv airport.

Desert Survival Skills

Sunday, June 28.

The pearlescent morning, coupled with Mark's enthusiastic anticipation of a day hiking the northern canyon of the En Gedi Nature Reserve, set a soft-focus lens over my obsession for online news of West Bank fighting, Qassam rocket strikes, and other evidence that *Let's Go* had given Mark a pitiful assignment. I woke up in an optimistic mood and decided to give in to the pleasure of that optimism. Besides, the night before, upon returning from a late afternoon drive with Mark across the Negev to two spectacular craters, Ha-makhtesh and Ha-makhtesh ha-gadol, and a stop in Arad for Chinese dinner at Mr. Shay (the *other* good restaurant in Arad), I had curled up in my usual spot in the lobby and thoroughly scoured the Internet—uncovering not one recent report of a Hamas-Fatah altercation or rocket launch from Gaza.

Today would include another "first" in this week of new experiences. Though we'd hiked together many times on family trips to Big Bend and the Colorado Rockies, this would be the first time Mark and I would hike as a duo, without Rex and Paul. I sat on my rumpled bed and studied the trail guide, map, and other information Mark had picked up in the reception area the night before, trying to get a clearer picture of what I was in for. The En Gedi Nature Reserve is an escarpment that descends two thousand feet to the Judean Desert on the western side and the Dead Sea on the eastern side. Two deep wadis cut through the rocky ridge, Wadi Arugot on the southern side and Wadi David to the north. The trails in the reserve were labeled "easy" to "very difficult." The northern canyon trail was described as "relatively easy," nothing like the thirteen-mile-loop hike of the south rim of the Chisos Mountains in West Texas, our family's New Year's Day tradition. But my lack of boots and appropriate clothing forced this concession. I'd have to make the hike in my stretchy black skirt and the walking shoes I bought for the trip. Though we'd be taking a "relatively easy" trail, hiking in our family was always an athletic event, and I was certain Mark would not be leading me on a leisurely stroll.

I looked over at Mark, who was moving at a deliberate pace as he gathered various items from the top of the dresser—a first-aid kit, a travel-size tube of sunscreen, a pocket-sized purple note-book, a camera, several protein bars—and put them in his day-pack. Turning my attention back to the information on the nature reserve, I found an entry describing the twentieth-century colonization of the area, reminiscent of news reports from the late 1940s in the *Sunday Ghibli*.

> On a rainy night on March 9th 1949, a company attached to the Alexandroni Division and commanded by Shmariya Gutman, a member of Kibbutz Na'an (and a part-time archaeologist) sailed on the Dead Sea from Sodom, intending to settle En Gedi in an attempt to include this location within the borders of the State of Israel. In

1953, a Nachal company (an army division consisting of pioneering fighting youths) settled on the land. Three years later the settlement turned into a kibbutz.

At the time Shmariya Gutman and his company arrived in this area, the land was home to Bedouins from the Rashida tribe, who cultivated their crops near the springs each winter.

Having completed his packing, Mark set aside two Nalgene bottles and a collection of other empty bottles. "We'll each need a quart of water for every hour of hiking," he said without looking up. Desert survival skills were completely internal to Mark these days, but I remembered when he'd first encountered those lessons. Planning for adequate water consumption was one of the first things he'd learned from his wilderness safety course with David Alloway, an expert on arid land survival techniques and author of the book *Desert Survival Skills.* At the time, Mark was a freshman at St. Stephen's High School in Austin and a member of the school's outdoor program. The group traveled to West Texas for a weeklong course with David, who met the students at their campsite in the Davis Mountains and set to work, undeterred by an injury he had recently sustained when a horse stepped on his foot. Two days into the course, however, David's foot was hideously swollen, and the group was forced to call for helicopter rescue. With David in a hospital in Midland, Texas, and the course cut short, the group bundled up their tents and gear and began their eight-hour drive back to Austin. Dr. Davis, head of the high school and director of the outdoor program, alerted parents of the early return. Late that afternoon, I gathered with other parents on St. Stephen's campus, outside the straw-bale hut that served as the outdoor program headquarters. When the small white school bus made its way up the winding, dusty trail toward us, I could see Mark's face framed by one of the large windows, a portrait rendered serious and sad. On the drive back to campus, Mark and the others had learned that David died. Apparently David, a virtual poster-man of fitness and health, had diabetes, a condition that left him with insufficient circulation to fight the infection from his wound. There was not a chapter in his book dealing with diabetes. These things just happened. And somehow, even though their contact was cut short by tragedy, David's death made his lessons all the more important to Mark.

Before departing for our hike, we stopped by the reception area to fill our empty bottles with cold springwater from the patio faucet. The water came directly from freshwater springs at the upper levels of the En Gedi Nature Reserve, which were fed by rainwater that seeped into the underwater table and welled up in the mountains. Much of three million cubic meters of water generated annually by the springs was captured and used by the kibbutz, whose members built a commercial plant to bottle the pure water. I wondered whether the Bedouins who had once occupied the land in the reserve had left because of dwindling access to water or simply because the neighborhood was no longer so welcoming. I didn't bring this up to Mark at the time because, frankly, I wanted our hike to be about nature, not Bedouins, and just spending time together.

In the car, we drove north toward the reserve on the road bordering the Dead Sea. According to my internal rating system, the heat again hit the charts a little above "unbearable," and I wondered how we'd fare hiking up the escarpment, even along a "relatively easy" trail. Mark had some welcome news: we wouldn't need to worry as much about getting sunburned or winded here as we would in Texas. "In the Dead Sea area the sun's harmful ultraviolet rays are filtered by thick atmospheric, evaporation, and ozone layers, so you can stay in the sun longer without burning," he read from a brochure he'd picked up at the kibbutz. "And the high barometric pressure—a result of being thirteen hundred feet below sea level—makes the air highly oxygenated so it's easier to breathe." I told Mark I wished the kibbutz could bottle this "atmospheric sunscreen" and ultra-oxygenated air so I could smuggle some home with me to Austin.

The first part of the hike was a dry, rocky path lined with acacias, jujubes, and balsams, small trees that provided little shade. The heat reverberated in visible ripples off the brown cliffs. Apart from the heat waves, the air was absolutely motionless and suffocating, and I struggled to fill my lungs. What was that again about hyper-oxygenated air? The canyon was soundless except for the crunching of limestone gravel under our feet and the occasional far-off notes of birdsong. We stopped briefly to drink springwater from one of the Nalgenes and noticed a group of teenagers off the path ahead, gathered around a tall, strikingly handsome young man. The teens appeared to be listening intently with their gazes firmly affixed on their virile guide. Mark said they probably were a "Birthright" group, one of the many groups of Jewish students from other countries who come to Israel to explore their Jewish heritage on an all-expense-paid trip sponsored by organizations like Amazing Israel or Jewalicious. Those, by the way, are honest-to-goodness real names. Several of Mark's friends had been on Birthright trips. "They pick out hunks and hunkettes to lead the tours," he told me, "which makes the kids *really* want to come back to Israel." (I later read several articles about Birthright confirming that this is, in fact, the group's modus operandi. One put it this way: "Crisscrossing the country in rollicking tour buses, Birthright participants between 18 and 26 swim in the Dead Sea, ride camels, visit the occupied Golan Heights, listen to lectures on Zionism and spend their nights boozing and flirting with the Israeli soldiers assigned to accompany them. . . . The common denominator of the Birthright experience is the promotion— by turns winking and overt—of flings among participants, or between participants and soldiers.")

Mark filled me in on the racy details of his friends' Birthright trips while we walked. The flat path we were on gradually turned into an uphill climb. Mark walked briskly, and I labored behind him up the trail, which wound upward and around the outcroppings of rough, mottled boulders. We emerged from the rocky corridor at a spectacular waterfall bordered by swaths of ferns. Mark set off with his camera to explore the caves and crevices cut into the limestone rock beyond the falls. I took off my new walking shoes and submerged my bruised and blistered feet in the cool, clear water. I sat there soothing my feet and watching the water percolate out of the canyon and splash into the rocky pool. Mark returned thirty minutes later, jotted down some notes in his small notebook and then took a dip in the pool. Wincing, I reluctantly stuck my feet back into my shoes before we began our descent.

Once down the canyon, we headed toward the archaeological site at the base of the escarpment to see the unearthed remains of an ancient Jewish community (the one Tom had told us about). So, had the Bedouins displaced the Jews or was it the other way around? Or had they coexisted peacefully for a time? I would try to remember to ask Tom if we ran into him again at dinner. On the way to the ruins, I slipped into the park store and bought a pair of bright blue flip-flops decorated with miniature Israeli flags. I tossed my new walking shoes in the trash. (At the time, I was thinking only of my throbbing feet, oblivious to possible future political implications. There would come a time later in our trip when I regretted displaying Israeli flags on my feet.)

When we returned to the kibbutz, I settled down in the lobby with "our" computer while Mark took "our" car and set out to research and review several Dead Sea-area hostels. Milling about in the lobby were a group of newcomers—an ultra-Orthodox Jewish group, judging by their dress. Watching discreetly, I was struck by the contrast between the men in the heavy, dark clothes and wide-brimmed black hats and the other hotel guests dressed in light summer clothing similar to what we would wear in Texas.

Back again to the computer. Among the email alerts from the *New York Times* was one with a link to an op-ed article about Israeli kibbutzim and settlements. The author suggested it was purposefully misleading for Israel to call the illegal housing areas it continues to construct in the West Bank "settlements" because the word "settlement" conjures up the image of a rural village, an image Israel wants to perpetuate in order to blur the reality that most of these housing areas are modern communities. (He pointed out that one settlement, Maale Aduim, spanned thirty thousand acres and had a population of thirty-five thousand.) But it was what he had to say about kibbutzim that captured my interest. In Israel, he said, the use of the term "settlement" originated with the kibbutzim. The author recalled when kibbutzim in Israel really looked like settlements:

> In the early 1960s, I spent time on Kibbutz Hakuk, a small community founded by the Palmah unit of the Haganah, the pre-state Jewish militia. Begun in 1945, Hakuk was just 18 years old when I first saw it, and was still raw at the edges. The few dozen families living there had built themselves a dining hall, farm sheds, homes and a "baby house" where the children were cared for during the workday. But where the residential buildings ended there were nothing but rock-covered hillsides and half-cleared fields.

Today, the author said, Kibbutz Hakuk makes its money from tourism and a plastics factory, and to refer to Hakuk as a settlement "would be bizarre." Reading the article, I was reminded of the mental image I'd had of a kibbutz before planning this trip. I'd pictured a community where men and women worked in the fields while others undertook communal domestic duties, and young children and babies were relegated to child care. I remembered my surprise when, in researching places to stay near the Dead Sea, I read that Ein Gedi Kibbutz operated a guesthouse, restaurant, and bar and featured an Olympic-size swimming pool—and when, after my arrival, I discovered the kibbutz also owned and operated a luxury spa and a commercial water-bottling plant. With its interests in tourism and bottled-water sales, Ein Gedi was quite different from my former conception of a kibbutz. I could see for myself that what the author said of Kibbutz Hakuk was true also for Ein Gedi Kibbutz—calling it a "settlement" would be absurd. (Later in the trip, Mark and I saw several of the Israeli settlements in the West Bank, and the author is correct: calling those modern housing areas "settlements" is definitely misleading.)

Back to my emails, I was delighted to see one from Rex and Paul. They'd spent the past few days in Juneau, Alaska. They went fishing for Dolly Varden trout in the Gastineau Channel but discovered it was the beginning of the pink salmon run, so they fished for salmon, hooking many and losing only a few to some very aggressive sea lions. Still nursing stiff shoulders and thighs from the Chilkoot Trail hike, they apparently had more time now to write. Rex reported that the packs he and Paul carried on the trek weighed well over forty pounds, far exceeding what they'd expected. They were in awe of their guide, Roger, from Packer Expeditions, who at all times kept a fast pace several yards ahead of them, belting out Broadway show tunes and exhibiting no signs of exertion from the eighty-five pounds of gear and provisions he carried in his huge backpack. "He completely dispelled any preconceived notions I may have had about guys with a penchant for musical theater not being mountain men."

The Salt Pillar of
Lot's Wife

The day after our hike, we saw a community that could be accurately described as a "settlement." When Mark completed his weekly copy batch for *Let's Go,* we drove south from Ein Gedi Kibbutz—past the northern basin of the Dead Sea, the Lisan Peninsula, Ein Bokek, and the "salt ponds" and peaks of white potash of Dead Sea Works. We turned off on a road that ran southeast through a long stretch of desert toward the southern Israeli-Jordanian border to our destination: Moshav Neot Hakikar, a small agricultural community set in the shadow of the Edom Mountains of Jordan. Fields of peppers, cherry tomatoes, watermelon, and dates surrounded modest houses, a community swimming pool, and a synagogue. Unlike a kibbutz, farms at a moshav are individually owned and operated. Mark said the sum of Neot Hakikar's tourism consisted of just a trickle of people. Some came to volunteer in the fields and stay in tents or cabins in the desert. Others came to hike, mountain bike, or visit the artists' quarter. We stopped in front of the bike rental shop, tucked in a house in the residential area, and Mark went inside to gather information for *Let's Go* about bike rentals and trails. I waited in the car. Looking around, I failed to locate even a trickle of tourists. Not one hiker, biker, or art enthusiast. Perhaps it was because of the heat. The sky was a white-hot bowl. The air had evaporated. I felt a brief sensation of guilty gratitude for the relative luxury of Ein Gedi Kibbutz, with its gardens fed by vast sprinkler systems and guests fed by sumptuous buffets.

Once Mark returned to the car, we headed back north and turned off the Dead Sea road, just south of the industrial area of Dead Sea Works, to see Mt. Sodom. The mountain, named for the biblical city, is part of a six-mile-long ridge of halite rising from an underground salt block. We drove to the top along a wide path cut in salty white sediment for automobiles (buses were prohibited) and got out of the car. The wind whisked across the crest where we stood alone, the only living things. A labyrinth of footpaths, tunnels, and surreal salt formations, formed by thousands of years of wind and rain, stretched before us. Mark loped off down a winding path, his body disappearing after the first curve, in search of a cave with chalk-white walls that he'd read about. I called out to him, fearing we'd be permanently separated, but soon realized the wind rapping the ridge and swirling through the tunnels made it impossible for him to hear me. With only the bright blue flip-flops on my feet, I set off behind him, plodding along the powdery limestone path that twisted through tunnels and over salt formations, continuing to yell his name. Then I heard the faint sound of his voice: "Follow the path to the right of the salt pillar of Lot's wife." God destroyed the cities of Sodom and Gomorrah because of the grievous sins of the people, but Abraham's nephew

Lot and his family were allowed to escape on the condition they not look back at the destruction. Lot's wife, distressed, no doubt, at walking away from her home and her neighbors, did look back, and promptly turned into a pillar of salt. Isn't looking backward supposed to be a worthwhile endeavor? Why on earth did I spend hours at the university studying history if not to understand the world in depth? Glancing around at the many configurations, I was puzzled. I couldn't imagine which most resembled Lot's wife. It was apparent I would never catch up with Mark.

Mark reappeared twenty minutes later, having retraced his steps back to the car to find me mildly panicked. A quick hug calmed my nerves. I did not realize it was so late in the day, but now the setting sun cast a purple hue on the hills. As we departed, Mark pointed out the pillar of Lot's wife. She stood alone, a bulbous-topped, oblong shaft separated from the surrounding rock. While Mark drove, I flipped through brochures about Dead Sea attractions and found a description of Mt. Sodom's "amazingly beautiful tunnels and caves," entrance to which "is forbidden due to danger of landslide." Perhaps the area was closed to visitors, but there was no sign indicating that it was off-limits. Would we have explored alone like that with the knowledge of such dangers? Sometimes there is no looking back. I was glad we stopped. I was even glad now for the small thrill of danger.

Back at the kibbutz, Mark and I had dinner at the guest restaurant. There was no one we recognized in the dining room so we had a quiet meal alone. Afterward, Mark went to the bar and I took the computer to the reception area. Opening the door to the lobby, I saw that a piano recital was taking place. Most in attendance were ultra-Orthodox Jews on retreat at the kibbutz. A partition divided the lobby, and men sat on one side, women on the other.

I quietly closed the door, took a seat on a bench in the outside corridor adjacent to the lobby, and opened the computer. With the weak, intermittent wireless signal, I got online and searched for news. Recent reports from the West Bank were not about gun battles or other skirmishes between Hamas and Fatah, but about clashes between Israeli soldiers and pro-Palestinian activists and between Jewish settlers and Palestinians. Near Ramallah, in the village Bil'in, pro-Palestinian activists had staged a demonstration against Israeli settlements, which were built on Palestinian land, and against the Separation Wall, which Israel constructed in the middle of the village's agricultural lands. The protestors claimed they were met with unprovoked tear-gas attacks by Israeli soldiers employing high-powered tear-gas cannons that propelled twenty-five gas canisters per second into the defenseless crowd. (Two months before, at a similar demonstration in Bil'in, Israeli soldiers had killed a Palestinian man with one of those tear-gas cannons.) Near Nablus, Palestinians claimed that Jewish settlers had raided a Palestinian village, fired guns at the windows of buildings, and injured two Palestinians. The Jewish settlers claimed Palestinians had started the incident by setting a fire at a nearby settlement and throwing stones at the settlers who were trying to douse the flames. One settler was injured. In Safa, a village near Hebron, several people were wounded when Israeli soldiers tried to prevent pro-Palestinian activists from accompanying Palestinian farmers to their agricultural fields. Activists claimed that Jewish settlers from a nearby settlement had continually attacked the farmers, and that they were only there to protect the farmers. Ignoring the evidence, the Israeli soldiers ejected the activists and told them the farm was a "closed military zone." Ramallah, Nablus, and Hebron, I noted with dread, were all on Mark's upcoming *Let's Go* itinerary.

As the piano concert came to a conclusion, I closed the computer and went to the bar to fill Mark in on all the turbulence in the West Bank. He was at a picnic table on the patio, talking to Zamir about military life, college, and most likely, the kibbutz's CD collection. I asked Zamir about the partition in the lobby, and he said it was to keep the ultra-Orthodox men and women from looking at each other while they listened to the music. He pointed out that the kibbutz had made other changes as well to accommodate this very conservative religious group, like arranging for separate swimming hours at the pool for men and women. Zamir laughed and said of the new group, "They are nuts." Then he quickly added, "But my family is Orthodox, and I'll probably get married in the Orthodox tradition, right down to the arranged marriage." Even after consuming a ridiculous amount of Goldstar, I could not, for the life of me, envision Zamir in a heavy black coat with peyot dangling beneath his hat, sitting on one side of a partition separating him from his wife . . . or anyone, for that matter.

Go in Peace and
Havahavahava Nice Day

While Mark slept in the dim room, I tiptoed into the bathroom. Standing before the large, rectangular mirror hanging over the sink, I couldn't help but smile. The stretchy black skirt and top, which I'd slept in every night for the past week, were, as advertised, wrinkle-free and looking remarkably good. Though the same was not true for my face (in retrospect, perhaps I should have purchased that Dead Sea mineral miracle cream while in Ein Bokek), there was little time to dwell on my appearance. Quietly, I put on my blue flip-flops, collected the laptop, opened the door, and stepped into another luminous morning at Ein Gedi Kibbutz.

Outside the guest cabins, housekeepers swept porches and pushed carts filled with crisply folded linens and fragrant fruit baskets. Gardeners pruned flowering bushes and adjusted drip irrigation hoses in garden beds. Men in black top hats and long black coats, clutching papers and books under their arms, walked along the paths from the cabins and across the sprawling baobab-shaded lawn to the reception area, where they congregated with their ultra-Orthodox colleagues along the corridor of meeting rooms outside the lobby.

I took a seat on a couch in the lobby. Across from me, a woman sat reading a worn leather-bound Torah. She was dressed modestly, similar to many other women in the reception area that morning. A black flowered scarf, poufy and tied around the back of her head, concealed the hair around her solemn face. She wore a white linen cap-sleeved blouse over a long-sleeved tee shirt with a high neck. A black skirt draped over her knees and upper calves. Thick white stockings covered her legs, and clunky white tennis shoes enclosed her feet. While looking at her, it occurred to me that the ultra-Orthodox dress code is much like ours in Western countries: men have a uniform—a suit, suitable for nearly all occasions. Women piece together various items of clothing depending on the occasion and season—which, in the case of ultra-Orthodox women, happens to be many pieces no matter what occasion or season.

I opened the computer. In two days Mark would begin his work in the West Bank. There were many news reports about the dramatic growth of the Jewish settlements there—an issue becoming increasingly more personal to me, having read many articles about violence between Jewish settlers and their Palestinian neighbors near areas on Mark's *Let's Go* itinerary. The Israeli government had just approved construction of fifty new homes in a West Bank settlement, which made the news because opponents considered the action a direct defiance of the Obama administration's call for a complete freeze on Israeli settlement building. Israeli Prime Minister Benjamin Netanyahu claimed the new construction was needed to accommodate the "natural growth" in the settlement (like grown children of settlers marrying and moving into their own homes), but opponents argued that the Israeli government was using "natural growth" as a cover to build more houses—and that most settlement growth was due to Jews from Israel or immigrants from abroad moving into the West Bank. One article I came across made me realize there was another dimension to the settlement issue: while the Israeli government was responsible for the establishment and growth of most West Bank settlements, some ultra-Orthodox Jews started settlements not condoned by—and in direct defiance of—the Israeli government. These settlers, believing that God gave Jews the right to all land between the Mediterranean Sea and the Jordan River (an area they call by the biblical names Judea and Samaria), were "fueled by religious fervor" and claimed "the Israeli government doesn't have the manpower or willpower to keep them out" of the illegal settlements.

After briefly pondering the problem of people acting outside the law to carry out the will of God, I turned my attention to something more mundane: our day's itinerary. Today we would be driving north of Ein Gedi Kibbutz to see a cliff-top guesthouse owned by Mitzpeh Shalem Kibbutz and a museum near the cave where the Dead Sea Scrolls were discovered. Our final stop would be at a cluster of private beaches along the northern coast of the Dead Sea.

In reading about the northern Dead Sea coast, I discovered the entire area is within the boundaries of the West Bank! How could that be? Mark had said nothing about going to the West Bank today. My heart slipped into "race mode" as I read on.

The northern Dead Sea coast is part of an area called the Jordan Valley, a strip of land ten miles wide and seventy-five miles long along the West Bank's eastern boundary. Reading on, I learned that the Jordan Valley is in Area C—the area under temporary Israeli military control and civil administration. Apparently the nature and extent of Israel's control and administration of the Jordan Valley were controversial and considered by some to be unfair, inequitable, and illegal. The Israeli human rights organization B'Tselem reported that Israel had accomplished a "de facto" annexation of the Jordan Valley by continuing to build Israeli settlements, preventing development in Palestinian communities, declaring most of the land "Israeli state land," and designating Israeli regional councils to govern the area. The sites on Mark's *Let's Go* itinerary for the day were in the jurisdiction of one of these Israeli regional councils—the Megillot Regional Council.

Mark appeared in the reception area, a bit disheveled, but he had his daypack over his shoulder, and I could see he was ready for the day. He said he hadn't mentioned that we'd be going to the West Bank today, but for good reason. "Traveling in the Jordan Valley is not much different from traveling in Israel." He went on to explain that we'd be driving on one of the many Israeli "bypass roads." The roads, which cut through the West Bank and bypass Palestinian areas, were built for use by the Israeli military, the Jewish settlers, and authorized visitors like us. We would be traveling only on protected roads and visiting only sights owned, operated, and secured by Israelis. We probably wouldn't even see a Palestinian. Mark's comments were confirmed by what I'd just read about the Jordan Valley, but still I wondered if I shouldn't stash a kef-fiyeh under my seat, just in case.

In the car driving north from Ein Gedi Kibbutz, I opened the map of Israel to find the exact boundaries of the West Bank, but there were none—the entire area looked like it was part of Israel. I looked out the window for the sign that would announce our crossing the internationally recognized Israel-West Bank border (the Green Line). Perhaps it would be something like "Watch out! You are entering the Palestinian territories!" But there was no such sign. We passed through an Israeli checkpoint, which had a guardhouse and a couple of armed soldiers who stopped us and asked about our nationality and destination. The checkpoint might have been set at the border between Israel and the West Bank, but it was so similar to the guardhouse at the Ein Bokek resort area that it just made me think we were heading to some posh beach resorts.

Our first stop was the Metzoke Dragot Holiday Village, a guesthouse owned and operated by Mitzpeh Shalem, an Israeli settlement and kibbutz located six miles north of the Green Line. The cliff-top guesthouse, which overlooked the Dead Sea, was set on a high, tapering precipice accessed by narrow switchbacks. Though the cliffs and ravines were popular with skilled hikers and climbers, the Holiday Village was marketed mainly to large groups from Birthright and other organizations. At the eastern edge of the small plateau, atop the cliff, was a reception area in a tiny stone building. We parked the car and got out to look around. There were, apparently, no visitors currently on holiday at this village. Mark went into the reception area to gather information for

Let's Go and then wandered around inspecting and photographing the odd arrangement of rustic, wood-frame structures—hostel-type rooms, classrooms, and a group cafeteria. I waited for him outside the reception area on a covered stone patio with wooden benches, iron lanterns, and a red hammock that swayed back and forth as the intermittent winds blew across the plateau. I imagined a bunch of American-Jewish teens, in Israel for the first time on a Birthright trip, relaxing on these benches and admiring the serene view and their hunkette leader. Would she tell them this area was within the Palestinian West Bank—part of the area designated to be part of a future Palestinian state? Or would she tell them this area was part of Judea and Samaria, land God gave to the Jews, and that it is their birthright?

Just north of Metzoke Dragot, we stopped at Qumran, the archaeological site where the Dead Sea Scrolls were discovered. From the audiovisual presentation in the museum, we learned that in 1946, a year before the UN voted to partition Palestine, a Bedouin shepherd found several clay jars containing ancient scrolls in a nearby cave. Hundreds of other scrolls were discovered in nearby caves during the following decade. The parchment scrolls, in Hebrew, Aramaic, and Greek, include the oldest biblical documents ever found, and many believe they were written by the Essenes, a Jewish sect that settled in this area more than two thousand years ago (though some attribute them to other groups).

From Qumran, we continued north along the Dead Sea road to the northern beaches. The route took us through an area that once was a Jordanian village but now was a bleak stretch of sand with the abandoned remains of the houses bombed by Israeli forces in 1967, during the Six-Day War. Mark pulled the car over to the side of the road and got out to photograph the rubble. I walked up to the charred, graffiti-covered exterior wall of one of the houses to get a closer look. There, scrawled in English and Arabic, was a tribute to its former inhabitants: "Tatane, Jibou, Naud, Gabi, Tabuse/Degling Family Rest in Peace." Portions of the exterior wall were gone. Inside, weeds grew among a mass of crumbled concrete, corroded pipes, and discarded trash. The only hint of how it may have looked when the Degling family lived there was, on one of the interior walls, a section of sky-blue patterned four-by-four tiles. Perhaps this was once a stylish kitchen, the hub of activity for the Degling family. Among the remains of the bombed-out houses, the village store stood intact except for windows and doors: a concrete building with cracked and peeling yellow paint and a sign over one doorway advertising Coca-Cola, which pictured a palm tree and the sun rising over a beautiful beach.

Just down the road from the bombed-out housing area, three separate private beaches protected by a wall of barbed wire stood adjacent to one another on the shores of the northern Dead Sea. The first beach, New Kalia, had an outdoor café with sofas shielded from the desert sun by a trellis of grapevines, an "authentic Bedouin tent," and a gift shop selling Dead Sea cosmetics. The nearby Biankini Beach seemed to aim for a quasi-Moroccan theme, with pillowed benches, hookah pipes, a restaurant serving Moroccan cuisine, a spa offering massages and beauty treatments, and both Bedouin- and Moroccan-style tents. The last of the three beaches, Neve Midbar, had more of a Sinai Desert ambiance, with palm-frond sunshades, a Bedouin tent, and Sinai-style thatched huts. The beach resorts had appropriated an Arabic atmosphere and were located in the Palestinian West Bank, but Mark said the Israeli military routinely barred Palestinians from using the beaches to appease Israeli settlers and tourists. A year or so after my trip to Israel and the West Bank, I came upon an article about a group of Israeli women who smuggled disguised Palestinian women through the Israeli checkpoint and into these beach areas to swim. There were even photos of the women, all swimming together and laughing in the water that was off-limits to half of the group. Though innocent on most every level, the women posed a real threat to the myths that spawned the "separation" in the first place.

Back in the car and leaving the beach area, we passed an Israeli sign set near the barbed wire separating the beaches from the bombed-out remains of the Jordanian neighborhood. On the sign, written in Hebrew, English, and Arabic, was the blessing "Go in Peace," words that echoed those Jesus offered to a sinner who had washed his feet: "Thy faith hath saved thee; go in peace." Mark turned on the navigation device, which when powered up, recited in its crisp British accent, "Have a nice day. Drive carefully." Mark rigged the device and it began rapping, "Havahavahava nice day. Dridridrive carefully. Havahavahava nice day. Dridridrive carefully." We started laughing, laughing at the navigation device, laughing despite ourselves at the juxtaposition of the private Israeli beaches and the bombed-out Jordanian houses and the irony of the Israeli beaches advertising authentic Bedouin tents being off-limits to Bedouins, laughing at the harsh, sad, disheartening reality of it all. We laughed as we'd done in the past at absurd cruelty jokes, if only to release our own anxieties. Our laughter was infectious, caught in a surreal self-amplifying feedback loop, and we simply could not stop laughing. And tears streamed down my face as the bombed-out ruins disappeared in the dust behind our generic yet trusty rental car.

Wisdom is Like a Baobab

Wednesday, July 1.

After breakfast, Mark sat cross-legged in an upholstered chair in the Ein Gedi Kibbutz guesthouse lobby, balancing the computer on his lap. Fanned out before him on a coffee table like an absurdly complicated poker hand lay the brochures and business cards he had collected from the northern Dead Sea beaches. A stack of other papers and a notebook filled with his reviews from the past few days sat hanging over the edge of the table, but within arm's reach. The next copy batch was not due to Mark's editor until the sixth of July, but he wanted to wrap up the Dead Sea chapter revisions before our departure the following morning. The only item remaining on his to-do list was a hostel and field school just north of the kibbutz, which he planned to see later in the day.

Also occupying the lobby were several of the ultra-Orthodox visitors. On one side, a man wearing a black top hat and suit sat alone reading a Hebrew newspaper. Three others in short-sleeved white shirts and *kippahs* (caps worn by Orthodox Jewish men) gathered in a corner, talking. All the men had full beards but no side curls. Did they belong to a sect of ultra-Orthodox Judaism different from that of the men with side curls who were on the flight with me to Tel Aviv? Perhaps before my trip's end I would more fully grasp the subtle distinctions among the sects. Across the lobby, two women sat on a couch, shoulder to shoulder, whispering to one another, their hair concealed by scarves and their bodies thickened by a panoply of colorless, layered clothing.

With Mark monopolizing my gateway to the day's news, I was left to my thoughts and my red Moleskine journal. Outside the reception area, I took a seat on the lawn in the cool shade of a baobab tree. Glancing over my journal entries for the past week, it occurred to me how dissimilar they were from those chronicling other trips I'd taken. In the past, I often included considerable detail about the historic sites I visited. But Mark wrote daily about that aspect of our travels and the information would soon be readily available in the revised edition of *Let's Go*. Now, I filled the lined pages with my observations about Mark and the sociopolitical issues that seemed to unfold continually before us—and on both subjects, my reflections were, without fail, interspersed with many questions.

I turned to an entry I'd made the night after our hike at the nature reserve. I'd written that it was becoming increasingly clear to me that Mark did not "need" me on this trip. What I knew to be true before setting out for this journey had been confirmed each day since my arrival. I hadn't, in any way, made this trip thinking Mark incapable of improvising in difficult or dangerous situations. It was true that I was motivated by fear for his safety, a fear that emanated from decades of headlines about terrorist attacks, rocket strikes, and suicide bombers—a fear that was, in my mind, validated by the US State Department warning against travel in the West Bank and one well-respected travel guide's suggestion to consider that entire area "off-limits." But honestly, how did I expect I might protect Mark in the event of a terrorist attack, rocket strike, or suicide bomber? Did I really consider this while planning the trip? Was my fear for Mark's safety some sort of unconscious pretense for my journey? Was there simply a part of me no longer willing to view the world through the filter of information or adventures relayed to me by the men in my life? Though there was an outside, slight, remote possibility that I'd capitalized on my safety concerns about Mark as an excuse to come to Israel, I had no regrets or reservations now about the trip. My curiosity about the region had already been brewing during the months before as I'd sorted articles from the *Sunday Ghibli.* And I was, frankly, having an incredibly satisfying experience with Mark.

And then there were the nearly overwhelming sociopolitical issues that seized my interest. I added one more question to the growing list in my journal, one that had come to me yesterday when Mark and I traveled north into the West Bank's Jordan Valley: The Israelis had a relatively secure existence in their own state with a thriving tourist, agricultural, and industrial economy, so why were they absorbing areas like the northern beaches of the Dead Sea we'd visited the previous afternoon, land designated for the future Palestinian state, but much of which was now off-limits to the population for which it was intended? If these beaches were the military "buffer zones" we so often read about, then they were the most decorated and trinket-laden buffer zones on earth. I, myself, could not do any serious sunbathing in an area meant to slow down terrorist incursions.

I closed my journal and joined Mark in the reception area. He was talking to a young woman whose thick, unrestrained black curls, form-fitting turquoise tee shirt, and extravagant hand gestures and smile set her apart from the others in the room. Victoria was Jewish, from New York. As a child, she had come with her parents to the kibbutz, a place she remembered as a paradise. Now on vacation with her husband, she was disappointed by what she called the "negative atmosphere" at the kibbutz, which she attributed to the somberness of the ultra-Orthodox group. "They are stuck in the past," she said. "It's as if they were living in nineteenth-century Poland." Then she turned to Mark and said something that both shocked and fascinated me: "Jews hate the ultra-Orthodox more than they hate Palestinians." While I had been fixated on the conflict between the Israeli and the Palestinians—and between Hamas and Fatah—I was now learning about another conflict, one between Jewish secular and ultra-Orthodox communities. Perhaps Zamir had alluded to this discord when he'd jokingly said of the ultra-Orthodox, "They are nuts."

After lunch, Mark left in the car to check the last item off his list, a hostel and field school near the En Gedi Nature Reserve. I'd seen enough tourist lodgings (and more than enough of our silver sedan), so I stayed behind.

Curious about Victoria's remarks, I searched online for information about "ultra-Orthodox Jews." I scrolled through several screens' worth of news articles and was surprised by what I read. The ultra-Orthodox lived by strict codes that governed how they dress, what they read, and how the sexes interact. In many ultra-Orthodox neighborhoods, rogue "modesty patrols" made sure residents adhered to those codes. They'd stoned a woman for wearing a red blouse, beat a woman for refusing to sit in the back of a bus, vandalized a pizza parlor for serving both sexes, and torched a store for selling devices capable of accessing the Internet, a source of pornography. "These breaches of purity and modesty endanger our community," said one ultra-Orthodox man. "If it takes fire to get them to stop, then so be it." The ultra-Orthodox had pressured the Israeli government for segregated buses and continued to operate a segregated bus, despite the government's effort to halt the publicly funded route. Ultra-Orthodox newspapers, prohibited from publishing pictures of women, even refused to print photographs of Israeli Foreign Minister Tzipi Livni when she won her party's leadership. The ban was like "something from the Middle Ages," said the Israeli Women's Network founder. "They are more conservative than Islamic fundamentalists who have no problems seeing women in public life."

Reading on, I discovered that the schism between the ultra-Orthodox and other Israeli Jews has existed since Israel was created—and has grown deeper with the growing ultra-Orthodox population. When Israel was created, only a small fraction of the population was ultra-Orthodox. The ultra-Orthodox rabbis were skeptical of Zionism, a movement focused on the creation of a national homeland for the Jewish people rather than the establishment of a religious theocracy. In return for ultra-Orthodox support of the secular state, David Ben Gurion, a Zionist and Israel's first prime minister, agreed to provide financial support to men desiring to pursue religious studies and to exempt them from military service. In addition, ultra-Orthodox rabbis were given governmental authority over life-cycle events like marriage and burial. Since 1949, the ultra-Orthodox population had grown significantly faster than the rest of Israel's population, and because most ultra-Orthodox men did not work and survived off allowances from the Israeli government, the ultra-Orthodox community had become a huge burden on Israel's economy. That, along with the substantial power they had in the government and their growing influence on Israeli society, had turned many Israelis against them. "It is not enough that they represent a public that participates in neither military service, the workforce—at least when it comes to most of the men—and the education system's core curriculum, they also have no qualms about demanding a foothold in the world of Israel's non-Haredi majority," said one Zionist about ultra-Orthodox Haredim efforts to expand the jurisdiction of rabbinical courts. "Liberals should defend their values and lifestyle from infringement by Haredim," one editorial said. "Haredi believe that, in the long run, they will take over the country."

The issues surrounding the ultra-Orthodox were more numerous and complicated than I had imagined. Did all the ultra-Orthodox feel so strongly about changing the Israeli culture? Were there "moderate" voices within the group? Were there secular Jews who defended the rights of the ultra-Orthodox, despite their differences? I came from a country that, even with some pockets of intolerance, allowed for a myriad of cultures to exist peacefully side by side. Was Israel moving toward or away from this model? I simply could not digest it all in one afternoon of reading.

After dinner with Mark, I waited outside the guesthouse restaurant for a night tour of the botanical gardens, one of many guided walks available to kibbutz guests. Mark passed on the tour. It was unlikely that any of his readers could afford to spend the night at the kibbutz guesthouse, and we were naturally and comfortably leading independent lives, even here where our journeys intersected. All traces of the sun had vanished below the horizon, and the deepening steel-gray sky silhouetted the tree boughs reaching out over the wadi. Branches ruffled with the warm breeze, their leaves reflecting a shimmer of moonlight. Two women, both wearing flowery shirtdresses and conservative pumps, joined me, and a few minutes later our guide, Zabu, strolled up to meet us, crunching out of the darkness from one of the kibbutz paths. He had a balding head, full white beard, bushy gray mustache, and thick glasses, and he wore khaki pants and a white tee shirt, much like Mark's hiking attire. Over his left hip was a leather satchel suspended from a shoulder strap that angled across his chest, and in one hand he held a heavy-duty flashlight. He appeared old, but not at all frail.

With Zabu in the lead, we began our garden walk. At the outset, I learned a couple of things about my companions. The two women were from France and were Orthodox Jews, but not ultra-Orthodox. Zabu was one of the founders of the kibbutz, and though I didn't know for sure, I imagined that he was one of the "pioneering fighting youths" of the Nachal Company who'd settled this land. From his dress, it was clear that he was not ultra-Orthodox, and from his comments, I could tell he was more Zionist/nationalist than religious zealot.

As we walked, Zabu pointed his flashlight at various trees and, in his charmingly imperfect English and thick accent, told us a little about each—a spindly turkey tree from India, a fast-growing rosewood from South America, a tropical "flamboyant" tree from Madagascar with fruit pods that are dried and used as traditional folk instruments, a native jujube called "Christ's thorn" because some believe Christ's crown was made from its branches. Zabu then showed us a tree he thought more beautiful than any other in the garden, a gargantuan multi-trunk ficus tree. The ficus, a very common houseplant, was easy to grow and nothing special, he told us, but this particular tree was quite special, an example of how something ordinary can become extraordinary: "A few house plants were planted here together in 1955, and then those plants united together in the garden and opened their branches and this is the result."

Zabu showed us one last tree, a baobab, the very one that had shaded me as I wrote in my journal earlier in the day. Its thick branches and massive trunk were illuminated by a ground-level floodlight, presenting a majestic conclusion to our tour. Zabu said the tree was brought to the kibbutz from Africa, where there are baobabs more than two thousand years old with trunks measuring nearly forty feet in diameter. Focusing his flashlight beam on one of the tree's colossal white flowers, he explained that they bloom only in the summertime, opening up just after sunset and at sunrise, and have a sweet nectar that attracts bats at night and bees at dawn. Stepping back and looking at the tree, Zabu announced proudly, "I call it the Obama tree because it was planted in 1960, same year President Obama was born." Then he added, "It's going fast—like Obama." Though Zabu meant to say, "It's *growing* fast," one of the two women quickly commented, "So Obama's 'going' fast? Hopefully it will be easy come, easy go for him." As she laughed, I looked down at the writing on a plaque set at the base of the tree:

Adansonia digitata "Baobab," Bombacaceae, Africa
"Wisdom is like a baobab: no-one can embrace it."
(African saying)
Plant—1960

The tour ended and Zabu disappeared into the night. As I walked slowly toward the café-bar to meet Mark, I thought there was nothing better than the baobab to exemplify the complexities of the region. The issues were simply too large for one person to embrace. As an outsider, I could not possibly understand all of the history, desires, fears, and aspirations of the Israeli people or the Palestinian people, much less their emotional ties to the land. Perhaps someday, but certainly not tonight. For now, I would have a beer with my son. I had already learned so much from just talking with Mark, who as it turned out, was a keen observer of the world around him. I had no doubt that I would now apply the metaphor of the baobab to all our coming days in Israel and the West Bank, and that I would think about it even longer.

Mark was sitting on the bench of our regular picnic table with a mug of Goldstar when I arrived. All the other tables were filled with guests—the busiest night at the café-bar by far since our arrival. Zamir delivered another Goldstar to our table, but his dual role as bartender and disc jockey kept him too busy for small talk. I told Mark about the tour of the botanical gardens and about

Zabu and the two trees. I repeated Zabu's comment that the bao-bab tree was "going fast" like Obama and repeated the woman's response, "Hopefully it will be easy come, easy go for him." Mark reminded me of our discussion a few days ago about the Jews who didn't like Obama because they believed he cared more about Palestinian statehood than about the future of Israel. Mark was well on his way to understanding many of the thorny issues we would encounter in our remaining days together in Israel and the Palestinian territories. I was just beginning.

Walking back to our room, we planned our early morning departure to Jerusalem so Mark could begin his work in the West Bank. "By the way," Mark mentioned, way too casually, "there was an incident in the West Bank today. Israeli soldiers shot at a bunch of Palestinian kids who were throwing rocks. A couple of the kids were seriously injured." Could I protect Mark if we were caught up in a group of stone-throwing Palestinians being shot at by Israeli soldiers? Probably not, but at least I'd be with him. Only a mother would take comfort in that.

Jerusalem, al-Quds

Thursday, July 2.

I opened the door of our cool and dimly lit room and stepped outside into one of my mother's watercolors: opaque, blue-violet sky brushed here and there with cloud-white, a backdrop to slender palms, shrubs exploding in red and tangerine flowers, expanses of smooth lawn. I remembered her series of Florida landscapes hanging in the entryway of her home facing the seventh hole of the Suntree Golf Course. She'd painted a dozen variations of this view in the back room of a Michael's store south of Orlando in her weekly class, "Paint with Bob." But the dry, hot air that hit my face as I opened our door, which hinted at the furnace that would temper our afternoon hours, reminded me that this was not balmy Florida. Before this trip, I would never have imagined the flora of tropical Florida thriving on a plateau near the Dead Sea. But just as European Americans eventually outnumbered the native Seminole and transformed their Florida swamplands into gardens, golf courses, and orange groves, the Zionist youth of the Nahal division took this rocky ridge where Bedouin nomads from the Rashida tribe once cultivated winter crops and converted it into a year-round garden oasis.

It was our last morning at Ein Gedi Kibbutz, and I went back into the room and retrieved my iPhone to take photographs of a spectacular date palm with fronds weighted down by clusters of firm, lime-green pods. The light and heat from our open door alerted Mark to morning's arrival. Soon, we had packed our belongings, checked out of the guesthouse, and begun our winding drive down the plateau. As the gardens of the kibbutz faded to rock and sand, Mark set the navigation device for the rental car return in downtown Jerusalem. Though Mark's remaining assignments with *Let's Go* required reviews in Palestinian-controlled areas in the West Bank, my concern about spending nights in those areas had prompted me to reserve a room at the Lutheran Guesthouse in Jerusalem's Old City. Our plan was to spend evenings in the Old City and take a bus to the Palestinian areas each day. Mark good-naturedly agreed to this arrangement for my benefit, though it would prove to be time-consuming (and the following week, when I returned home, he quickly gathered his belongings and moved to one of those Palestinian-controlled areas).

Our hour-and-a-half drive from Ein Gedi to Jerusalem took us on interconnecting Israeli bypass roads through the Palestinian West Bank, a journey of socioeconomic contrasts. Just past the turnoff for the northern Dead Sea beaches, the sleekly black-topped and highly secured Israeli highway cut through a stretch of sparsely populated desert. We passed an elderly Bedouin in traditional dress standing alone with his camel near a sign advertising camel rides and photographs. (We later learned that the Bedouin was a former livestock herder from the Jahalin tribe who was in the tourist trade because he no longer had access to land for grazing his herds.) Farther west, we passed a sparse Palestinian village on a bleak brown hillside, a village that consisted of a few meandering dirt paths, a scattering of tents and tumbledown shacks made of corrugated steel and plywood, and a couple of donkeys. A young woman wearing a *hijab* (a veil worn by Muslim women) and long brown dress cradled a baby in her arms as she walked along a sandy path near the expressway. Her hijab fluttered wildly behind her each time a car or tour bus sped by. Approaching Jerusalem, we saw Ma'ale Adumim, the Israeli settlement I'd read about a few days before, which covers an area one and a half times that of New York City. It was a surprising, unexpected sight in this otherwise barren landscape. The settlement's modern houses, side by side, one after another, coming into view for miles, shot up from the hilltops as though they'd simply sprouted after a brief desert shower and might recede again shortly into the ground. They were indeed some sort of protected desert garden, surrounded by three tiers of towering stone walls erected by the Israeli settlers to insulate them from their Palestinian neighbors.

We said goodbye to our rental car and our navigation device on the western side of Jerusalem, a modern area with high-rise office buildings, upscale restaurants, and grand hotels, and took a cab to Jerusalem's Old City. From this point of our journey on, we would travel by taxi or public transportation. The driver dropped us at the Damascus Gate, and I followed Mark through the passageway into the ancient walled city, he lugging his backpack and me pulling my roller bag, which bumped along with a jazzy rhythm over the uneven cobblestones. We made our way slowly, treading carefully on the rounded stones, through the crowded Arab marketplace along Souq Khan as-Zeit, a narrow street lined with shops displaying the usual candy, cigarettes, postcards, and tee shirts. But there were also baskets full of fruits and vegetables, huge bins of aromatic spices, pastries on brass trays, sequin-embellished *bedlah*, red and black keffiyehs. A constant, low hum of Arabic, Hebrew, and European languages softened the occasional shouts of eager vendors. Shoulder to shoulder, we walked beside Arab boys in tee shirts and jeans, Muslim women in hijabs and long dresses, ultra-Orthodox Jews in black hats and heavy jackets, Franciscan monks in dark hooded robes, American tourists in shorts and straw hats. At one point, our passage was temporarily blocked by a half-dozen Israeli police mediating a loud dispute, which involved a great deal of waving arms between an Arab shop owner and a young ultra-Orthodox Jewish man. Nearing the end of Souq Khan as-Zeit, we turned off on a side street and climbed a narrow set of thick, stone stairs, gently worn by more than a century of footsteps, to the Lutheran Guesthouse.

The Lutheran Guesthouse was set at a high point in the Old City, not far from the intersection of the city's four quarters: Muslim, Christian, Armenian, and Jewish. We found the entrance to the guesthouse in an arched stone alcove and announced our arrival via a speakerphone. The hammered metal doors opened to a sunlit lobby with a domed ceiling and the welcome of a young Arab desk clerk, Yousef. The iron lanterns, walls of smooth stone, and arched windows, doors, and niches gave the place an Old World look, while the simple furnishings of our room mirrored those at Ein Gedi Kibbutz: two narrow twin beds and a wooden desk. If Mark's eyes swept the room for a basket of fruit like the ones we'd enjoyed each day at the kibbutz, he did not mention it. My son and traveling companion was completely accepting of any situation we found ourselves in. And this was, after all, not an industrial hangar.

Before leaving the guesthouse to investigate more of the marketplaces and winding alleys, we stopped in the study, a spacious second-story room with expansive views of the Old City. Among the many things on Mark's to-do list was arranging a meeting with a program coordinator at the Siraj Center for Holy Land Studies in the West Bank. Mark had heard about George from the American professor he'd shared a cab with from the Israeli border to Petra, the same professor who had cautioned him about inspections and confiscations at Israeli checkpoints. The professor described George as "an all-around amazing person" who could give Mark a good introduction to the West Bank. Mark reached George on the first call, and they planned to meet at the Siraj Center's office in Beit Sahour, a village near Bethlehem, the following afternoon.

While Mark studied bus schedules and maps in anticipation of tomorrow's meeting, I scanned the tourist information displayed on the coffee table. In addition to learning about the Lutheran Guesthouse (the building was designed by Conrad Schick, a German architect who had settled in Palestine in 1850, and was set on the foundation of a Crusader edifice dating back to the eleventh century), I came across a leaflet advertising tours of the Old City. Curious, I called to inquire about the possibility of taking a tour the following morning, before departing for Beit Sahour. "Do you want a Christian or a Jewish tour?" the operator asked. I decided on a Christian one and arranged to meet up with a guide early the following morning. Then I dropped into a chair near Mark and listened as the *Adhan* (the Muslim call to prayer) echoed from the Old City's mosques.

Though not devout, we are Christian, which is why I spontaneously opted for the Christian tour. I was baptized in the Roman Catholic Church. As a child, I went with my mother and sisters to weekly confession and repented my sins by reciting a string of Hail Marys and Our Fathers to the count of the opal beads on my rosary. We attended mass and took communion faithfully every Sunday. For my confirmation, I chose Elizabeth, the cousin of Mary, as my patron saint and added her name to mine. I don't recall why I selected St. Elizabeth over the others, but I do remember liking the alliteration (my middle name is Elaine). It wasn't until I later read the Gospel of Luke that I fully grasped the nature of her sainthood: she had conceived a child at an "advanced" age, a miracle made possible by an angel who answered her husband's prayers for a son. Church was one of the many family activities that did not include my father, who was often on TDY (temporary duty assignment), flying planes to far-off places. When home on a Sunday, he preferred reclining in his La-Z-Boy and reading the newspaper to sitting in a church pew listening to a sermon.

Rex, my husband, was raised in a conservative fundamentalist church, the Northside Church of Christ in Richmond, Indiana. While in high school, he spent Sunday mornings entertaining Northside's four-to-eight-year-old Sunday schoolers with the harmonica, guitar, and Bible stories. Mark and Paul were baptized at First Presbyterian Church in Houston. When they were young, our family moved to Austin, where we attended Sunday services at Covenant Presbyterian Church or held "family church" at home, with Rex playing the harmonica and guitar and telling Bible stories just as he had done at Northside. While at St. Stephen's Episcopal School during middle school and high school, Mark and Paul attended daily chapel service and took required courses in comparative religion and theology. Sometime in early adolescence, the boys announced unequivocally that this was enough religious instruction, and Rex and I acquiesced.

It was during their middle-school years that both Mark and Paul started questioning organized religion. With so many different beliefs and conflicting views, how could any one religion be the "right" one? And what about evolution? Those questions and more prompted many lively dinnertime debates and led to a somewhat controversial business endeavor that took off during Mark's freshman year of high school. On the drive home from a day of fishing with Rex, it was ten-year-old Paul who noticed there was a theological war, of sorts, taking place on the backs of cars in Austin. Some cars proudly displayed the Christian fish symbol, while others bore parodies of the symbol, like a fish symbol with legs and the word "Darwin" to represent evolution. Other cars sported a fish symbol with the word "Gefilte" to represent Judaism. And some cars even had symbols responding to the parodies, like one with a "Truth" fish devouring a "Darwin" fish. Over dinner that night, Paul said the fish symbol reminded him of fishing, and he suggested that people of all religions, along with agnostics and atheists, would be better off if they set aside their theological differences and spent a day fishing together. The discussion rapidly evolved into a business plan: Paul and Mark designed a fish decal with the words "5 LB. BASS," which (with a little parental seed money) they promoted as the fishermen's response to the theological battle. When *Austin American-Statesman* humor columnist John Kelso wrote an article about Paul and Mark's "fishy business," as he called it, sales skyrocketed and so did emails, most from people who loved the decal, a few from those who didn't. One woman wrote that the decal mocked the very foundation of Christianity and warned: "Just remember you will one day stand before God. I sure wouldn't want to have that on my soul." The boys wanted to respond that they didn't stick their decals on *souls*, just bumpers.

Although I had instinctively selected the Christian tour, part of me now wished I'd opted for the Jewish tour, so we could have learned more about their faith. Or perhaps a Muslim tour.

Mark gathered his papers and maps, and after a brief stop to drop them off in our room, we walked through the heavily shaded alleys of the Old City's Christian Quarter, browsing stalls filled with tourists and knickknacks: Jerusalem stone crosses, Holy Land crystal rosaries, Jordan River holy water, olive wood nativity scenes, Virgin Mary pendants, bronze crucifixes, biblical incense, patron saint medallions, guardian angel night lights, Last Supper wall plaques, and more.

We stopped to eat at a tiny restaurant, where I discovered a brochure tucked in the menu, "Jerusalem, al-Quds, Capital of Arab Culture, 2009." On the cover was a sepia-toned photograph with a distant view of the minarets of mosques and the domes of cathedrals rising above the stone walls of Jerusalem's Old City. In the foreground, sheep grazed on patches of grass, watched by a lone Bedouin shepherd in a white turban and flowing white robe, strikingly similar to my memories of the nomads who temporarily occupied the land just beyond the back gate of my childhood home in Tripoli. The brochure contained the details of the yearlong program, initiated by UNESCO and implemented by ALESCO (the Arab League), of festivals, seminars, exhibitions, and other activities to highlight the importance of al-Quds (the Arabic name for Jerusalem) to Arab history and culture. It opened with a statement about the importance of Jerusalem to many cultures and religions:

> Al-Quds–Jerusalem is the dawn of civilization and the nourishing cradle of history. The city destined to be the cradle of the prophets, of divine religions and ancient civilizations: the land of peace that accommodates mosques' minarets and church bells. This is the city whose walls, gates, streets, houses, and people reflect diverse dynasties and cultures. It is on this land that civilizations took the first step toward enlightenment, a path with intertwined cultural, spiritual, and human dimensions. The history of Jerusalem reflects how the city was always cherished and referred to as the spirit of the homeland.

It went on to emphasize the spiritual, cultural, and political importance of Jerusalem to Palestinians, which remained "despite all Israeli Occupation attempts to subjugate its Palestinian citizens and their Arab identity." I told Mark what I'd read. The UN plan for partition of Palestine envisioned Jerusalem and Bethlehem as international cities to be administered by the United

Nations. The Green Line set out in the Armistice Agreements that followed the 1948 Arab-Israeli War divided Jerusalem: on the Jordanian side of the Green Line was the West Bank, which included Jerusalem's Old City. Israel had captured the Old City along with the rest of the West Bank in 1967 and has occupied it since that time. Mark said that both Israelis and Palestinians considered Jerusalem their capital. Israel proclaimed Jerusalem as its capital, though no country recognized the action, and the Palestinians proclaimed East Jerusalem, which includes the Old City, to be the capital of their future state. "Jerusalem is important to all faiths," Mark concluded, "too important to be a political symbol or a tool for negotiation."

After dark, we walked back to the guesthouse. The shops along Souq Khan as-Zeit Street were shuttered and shoppers gone. The streets were silent save the occasional radio music seeping out with the faint light from barred windows. Back at the Lutheran Guesthouse, I stopped in the lobby to check the news reports from the West Bank. I discovered several articles about the Israeli soldiers who'd shot at a group stone-throwing Palestinian youths yesterday in the West Bank, the incident Mark had so casually mentioned last night. The Palestinians "youths" were children, all under the age of sixteen. They had been throwing stones at civilian vehicles on a road near Nablus when the Israeli soldiers opened fire. Of the four who were struck, two were seriously injured. The Israeli soldiers had used live ammunition.

Here, of the Virgin Mary, Jesus Christ Was Born

Friday, July 3.

I was lured out of dreamless sleep by the sound of Jerusalem's mosques exhaling the morning's first Muslim call to prayer. The sky wove invisible threads of sacred sound over the ecru minarets and muted silver domes of the Old City as I stood at the window of our guesthouse room. The sound was soothing. Already I had a small sense of a life lived within the rhythm of scheduled prayer. Mark was awake now, too, and both of us inclined toward silence as long as the Adhan continued. After breakfast, we made our second venture into the depths of the Old City. The narrow alleyways seemed filled with even more detail, more color than the afternoon before. Intricately embroidered fabrics and Oriental carpets hung from low awnings of shops, sheltering workers from the morning sun. Shopkeepers set up stalls, arranging silver, pewter, and antiques. Elderly women in long black dresses, hijabs snug around deeply creased faces, spread blankets on the ground and arranged lettuce leaves, artichokes, and eggplant. Young girls made their way swiftly along the cobblestones, balancing on their heads boxes of apples, tomatoes, and mangos. Merchants shouted in Arabic over the clinking of tins and cracking of crates as they filled vats of pickles and olives and bins of nuts and spices. The faint morning breeze smelled of cumin and allspice.

Our guide, Ram, was short and balding underneath his floppy tan hat. Clenching a plastic bag containing three water bottles and assorted fresh fruit, he led us along the Via Dolorosa, a path through the Old City that Jesus is said to have walked while carrying the cross from his condemnation by Pontius Pilate to his crucifixion. Along the way, Ram reverently pointed out the Stations of the Cross, stopping at each site to recount, in his pleasant but businesslike manner, the stories of Jesus's suffering. Our final stop was the Church of the Holy Sepulchre, the most holy of the Old City's Christian shrines, where we joined a progression of pilgrims and filed in to view the rock that held the cross on which Jesus was crucified (the Rock of the Calvary) and the tomb marking the site of Jesus's burial (the Sepulchre). Several Christian denominations shared ownership of the church and held services in the dozens of ornate chapels housed within it. During the Ottoman era, because of the rivalry between Christian factions, the keys to the church were entrusted to two Muslim families, and to this day, descendants of these families continue to open the church's doors each morning and padlock them each night.

At the conclusion of the Via Dolorosa, Ram, a Christian Arab, hesitantly agreed to take us to one Jewish site, the Western Wall. It was Mark's suggestion, but I enthusiastically joined in the request. The Western Wall is on the western side of the Temple Mount, one of the most important and contested religious sites in the Old City. The Temple Mount, known to Muslims as Al-Haram

Al-Sharif, is considered one of the holiest sites in both Islam and Judaism. Israel took control of the Temple Mount when it captured the Jordanian-held Old City and the rest of the West Bank during the Six-Day War in 1967. The Israeli government agreed to let the Islamic Wadf, who had managed the Temple Mount for centuries, continue to manage the site. Meanwhile, Israeli bulldozers razed an entire Arab neighborhood adjacent to the Western Wall in order to build a stone courtyard that would serve as an open-air synagogue for Jews.

Ram waited patiently just outside the entrance to the Western Wall with other Arab guides, and from the back of the courtyard I watched as Mark took a paper kippah from a basket on a table and joined the other men and boys who wrote prayers on paper scraps and wedged the folded papers between the stones in the sixty-foot-high wall. There were no women praying with the men who stood along the vast majority of the wall, so I didn't accompany Mark. I later learned that Israeli law prohibits women from praying with men at the Western Wall and that women have their own, albeit much smaller, designated praying area. Watching Mark, I recalled the uproar the year before when a yeshiva student dislodged President Obama's prayer note from the stones and the prayer was printed on the front page of an Israeli newspaper. After securing his note in a safe niche, Mark stood at the wall, still and quiet, contemplating the ancient ritual as the ultra-Orthodox men on either side of him rocked back and forth with their prayer books. Looking at Mark, in his Hawaiian-style flowered board shorts and a brown tee shirt, with both a red paisley bandana and white paper kippah on his head, I felt certain that his prayer note, no matter how insightful, would not be the target of any impertinent yeshiva student. If the God of Israel had a playful side, he would be very curious about a note from a young man dressed with such abandon from the other side of the world—a note perhaps praying for people to set aside their theological differences and spend a peaceful afternoon together fishing.

The tour concluded, and we bid farewell to our solemn guide. Mark and I walked the short distance to the Damascus Gate, where we emerged from the Old City into the glare of modernity and the honking and screeching of cars on Sultan Suleyman, the street that would lead us to the Arab bus station. In Jerusalem, there was an Arab bus station and an Israeli bus station. An Arab bus was required for travel to Palestinian-controlled areas in the West Bank, and an Israeli bus for travel to places in Israel or to Israeli settlements and other Israeli-controlled areas in the West Bank. The same was true of taxis and tour guides. We were going to Bethlehem, an area designated Area A and under the security and civil control of the Palestinian Authority, so we boarded a bus at the Arab station. There were just a few others on the bus: in one seat, a woman with graying hair covered loosely with a hijab, and in another, two teenaged girls sitting side by side conversing in Arabic. There were no Israeli Jews on the bus. They were, as Chaim had informed me in his email, prohibited by Israeli military order from traveling to Palestinian-controlled areas in the West Bank, including Bethlehem.

As the bus headed toward Bethlehem, six miles southeast of Jerusalem, I glanced down at my bright blue flip-flops, the ones I'd purchased at the En Gedi Nature Reserve park store—the ones with little Israeli flags. *Lonely Planet's* admonition flashed in my mind: while in Palestinian-controlled areas, try to look like a Palestinian sympathizer. Yikes! I was on a bus bound for an area under the security and civil control of the Palestinian Authority, and my feet were adorned with Israeli flags! I started frantically scraping off the potentially offensive symbols with my fingernails. Mark stared at me for a moment and then laughed out loud when I said I needed to get the flags off before we got to the West Bank. "Mom, we're already in the West Bank." He reminded me that the Old City and East Jerusalem were in the West Bank, though Israel has been occupying those areas and the rest of the West Bank since 1967.

Approaching Bethlehem, the bus jerked to an abrupt stop. Out the window, I saw a blockade of armed Israeli soldiers. It was another Israeli checkpoint, though nothing like the small guard-house with a couple of soldiers we'd passed through at the Israeli resort Ein Bokek, or like the one along the Israeli bypass highway between Ein Gedi Kibbutz and the northern Dead Sea beaches. The checkpoint was a massive structure of concrete, steel, and barbed wire. On the top of the building, soldiers armed with Uzi submachine guns scanned the ground below. As our Arab driver motioned us to exit the bus, I brushed the pile of miniature Israeli-flag crumbs to the floor beneath my seat. I followed Mark to the checkpoint's huge wire holding pen, where we were herded from one area to the next by remotely operated doors, one opening after another as we passed through. We were questioned by expressionless Israeli soldiers who sat behind bulletproof glass, spoke via speakerphones, and inspected the travel documents we slid through narrow slots in the thick glass. Any of these soldiers could have, at one time, been our friend Zamir, though I could not picture him here in this harsh, cold environment. The whole scene, monitored by ceiling cameras, transported me back to my first and only trip to the renowned "Wallis Unit," the Texas State Penitentiary in Huntsville. While clerking for the chief judge of the US District Court in Houston, I had been assigned to interview a prisoner who had filed a First Amendment case against prison officials. It had been my first job out of law school. Years later, I could still feel the clammy, claustrophobic tingle in my arms and stomach that I'd felt then as the metal doors slammed behind me. Even Mark seemed less calm and relaxed than usual.

Having satisfied the guards' scrutiny, we exited the doors of the Israeli checkpoint on the Bethlehem side, where we each took a cleansing breath and then found a throng of Palestinian taxi drivers desperately seeking our patronage. Mark negotiated with several of the drivers and hired the one offering the best deal to take us to Bethlehem's Manger Square. As our taxi rolled out of the parking lot, I turned to look back at the Israeli checkpoint. On either side of the building, the towering thirty-foot-high concrete wall crowned with razor wire stood as a menacing backdrop. This was the Separation Wall, which figured largely in so many of the articles I had read lately. Israel claimed the wall was necessary to keep terrorists out of the country. Now I was even more confused. If the boundary between Israel and the West Bank, the Green Line, was in Jerusalem, why were the Israeli checkpoint and Separation Wall *within* the West Bank? Mark explained that Israel had "unilaterally annexed" East Jerusalem (which includes the Old City), along with an additional sixty-four square kilometers on the West Bank side of the Green Line that belonged to twenty-eight Palestinian villages. "Israel treats these areas as its own. That's why Israel erected the checkpoint and the Separation Wall well inside the West Bank. But no other country recognizes any part of the West Bank as being part of Israel."

I turned my attention to the road we were traveling on to the site believed to be the birthplace of Jesus. The taxi took us along Manger Street, a modern road curving around Bethlehem's broad hills, toward Manger Square. Arabic hip-hop played on the radio, my hair blew in the breeze, and my mind was a jumble of conflict and ironies. Why was I not eagerly anticipating my visit to Bethlehem, the city I had read so much about in the small white Bible presented to me at my confirmation? I had anticipated the emotion, the awe I would feel on the drive to the city that Christians worldwide held to be the cradle of Christianity. Instead I thought about the inhospitable structure looming over the city: the colossal checkpoint, the towering wall, the armed and edgy Israeli soldiers. What happened to "Oh little town of Bethlehem, how still we see thee lie"? What right did Israel have to build the checkpoint and wall on Palestinian land that was designated to be part of a future Palestinian state? I looked over at Mark, whose thoughts were elsewhere. A street map of Bethlehem lay unfolded in his lap with an assortment of brochures and guidebooks.

Our taxi rolled to a smooth stop around the corner from Manger Square, a stone plaza bordered by the Basilica of the Nativity on one side and the Mosque of Omar, evidence of Bethlehem's growing Muslim population, on another. (During the

1948 Arab-Israeli War, hundreds of thousands of Muslims were forced or fled from their villages in areas captured by Israelis, and thousands of those refugees settled in and around Bethlehem, which at the time was predominantly Christian.) Nearby, Palestinian cab drivers huddled, smoking cigarettes and talking, by a row of battered orange taxis. There were few tourists. I suspected many Americans had been scared away from Bethlehem by the US State Department's advisory against traveling in the Palestinian territories—and by guidebooks like *Frommer's*, which omitted the entire section on the Palestinian territories and warned readers to "consider this area off-limits." The only Americans we saw arrived on a tour bus from Jerusalem, which waited with its engine running while passengers were shuttled off the bus and across the street for a quick tour of the Basilica.

The Basilica of the Nativity was more fortress than cathedral, a plain stone facade with windows completely sealed long ago as a safeguard against intruders. For fourteen centuries it withstood conquests, insults, religious turmoil, and reform. But nothing in its history prepared the basilica for the present-day struggle and the technologies that propel the deadly argument forward. In 2002, in the wake of the Second Intifada (the Palestinian uprising from 2000 to 2005 against the Israeli occupation), Israeli forces launched a major military offensive on Bethlehem in search of Palestinian militants. Israeli tanks surrounded the courtyard. Israeli snipers positioned on rooftops besieged the Basilica with gunfire, killing nine militant Palestinians who were hiding inside with innocent Palestinian civilians and monks and the church's bell ringer. Gently touching the scars in the stone left by the bullets, I had a visceral sense of the recent history of conflict. It was not at all what I had expected to find when I began this journey. All of my preconceived notions of the region's danger had been upended.

The basilica's entryway, scaled down centuries ago to prevent intruders from entering on horseback, was so low Mark and I had to crouch to enter. Inside the church, the air was cool. Limestone columns in the open nave, absent of pews, framed the sanctuary. Beneath the altar, a set of worn stone steps wound down to a small cave. At the time of Jesus's birth, many of Bethlehem's peasants lived in structures built above grottos where they kept their flocks. This was believed to be one of those grottos, the one where Mary and Joseph stayed the night of Jesus's birth. The musty air in the cave smelled of stale incense, the interior dimly lit by a strand of bulbs. A silver star was set in the worn marble floor, and on it an inscription in Latin: *Here, of the Virgin Mary, Jesus Christ was born*. This was the place where Christians from all over the world came to pray and rejoice the birth of their savior. Not so long ago, I might have believed this place to hold the power to heal the wounds that past decades inflicted on these people. My time in Israel and the West Bank had dismantled that sort of magical thinking.

In the faint light of the grotto, Mark jotted notes in his purple notebook labeled "Bethlehem." I closed my eyes and prayed. I prayed that there would be peace in Bethlehem, at least for today, and that Palestinian boys angry about the continued presence of the Israeli military and Jewish settlers weren't lobbing stones and provoking the Israeli guards.

From the church, we walked to the Bethlehem Peace Center, which also faced Manger Square. The Peace Center, a two-story open and airy building built and operated by the Swedish government, offered maps, guides, and other useful information about the Palestinian territories. Mark gathered phone numbers and operating hours for local emergency services, banks, post offices, and other government services. I picked up a copy of *This Week in Palestine*, a glossy color booklet that highlighted information about, and upcoming events in, the Palestinian territories. There were two full pages dedicated to statistics, such as the average net daily wages for males ($19.80 USD), percentage of households below the poverty line (57.3 percent), and hotel occupancy rates (22.1 percent). Bleak statistics notwithstanding, the information in the other pages was surprisingly upbeat and optimistic. There was a complete directory of Palestinian hotels, restaurants, and museums, and an impressive calendar of Palestinian film, dance, and music events. Among several articles about sights in the West Bank was one about Israel's Separation Wall:

> The Wall that Israel has erected around the West Bank and that encircles Palestinian cities and towns has become an attraction in itself, a site to be visited and to marvel at—aghast. All sorts of graffiti have popped up on it, and it has become the backdrop for cultural activities, concerts, and fashion shows.

The West Bank was, to repeat Chaim's words about Israel, a very "with it" place.

Come and Celebrate
Palestine

At midday, Mark and I stepped out of the heat and into Afteem, a traditional Palestinian restaurant around the corner from Manger Square, where we shared a giant plate of hummus and falafel. After devouring every morsel, we began walking toward George's office in Beit Sahour. The walk took us, in Mark's words, "well beyond the line that well-intentioned religious pilgrims never cross." We abandoned the tourist circuit and followed a narrow road hedged by white limestone buildings, arched passageways, and oleanders heavy with pink blossoms. The road sloped down to a clutter of apartments and office buildings and, beyond that, a rocky field illuminated by the sun in hues of apricot and tangerine. This was the place Christians believed to be Shepherds' Field. Although tourists frequently traveled to Beit Sahour to see the field where an angel is said to have announced the birth of Jesus to the shepherds, most arrived on sightseeing buses and departed swiftly after touring the biblical sites.

Mark led the way and displayed no visible concern as he ventured deep into the recesses of this Palestinian village to meet a person he'd heard of once, and only by chance. I, on the other hand, consciously reminded myself to unknit my eyebrows and breathe more than once. Watching Mark, Rex's maxims "when in doubt, go for it" and "nothing is more energizing than purposeful activity" echoed in my head. These sayings had guided every family vacation we'd taken since Mark was a toddler. It occurred to me that the very fact of our being on this particular journey demonstrated how fully ingrained they were in Mark, just as they already were a few years back when Rex included them as the "top two" on a laminated list he presented to our college-bound son:

10 THINGS I WISH I KNEW EARLIER
FATHERLY ADVICE ON THE OCCASION OF
MARK'S DEPARTURE FOR HARVARD
September 2006

1. WHEN IN DOUBT, GO FOR IT. People so often regret the opportunity that passed untaken. Rarely do they regret accepting challenges.

2. NOTHING IS MORE ENERGIZING THAN PURPOSEFUL ACTIVITY, and its corollary, ACTION IS BETTER THAN INACTION. People become listless, apathetic, and fatigued when they are unchallenged. The cure is to throw yourself into an activity that requires energy and focus.

3. LEARN PEOPLE'S NAMES AND FACES. Everyone likes hearing their own name. This takes a little concentration, but make it a habit.

4. FIRST IMPRESSIONS ARE FOREVER. Make a good one.

5. DON'T IRRITATE PEOPLE UNNECESSAR-
ILY. Sometimes it feels good to humiliate or embar-
rass someone who has mistreated you. It is hardly ever
worth it, and it will come back to bite you.

6. LEARN TO DANCE. Foxtrot, swing, waltz. A
little competence will make you so much more comfortable and poised when you need to dance, and you
will need to dance.

7. IT TAKES THE SAME AMOUNT OF TIME TO
THROW AWAY THE PIZZA BOX WHETHER
YOU DO IT NOW OR NEXT THURSDAY. The
only difference is whether you spend a week with a
roach-infested cardboard box on your coffee table.

8. DISORGANIZATION IS THE GREAT TIME-
WASTER. This is counterintuitive, but making to-do
lists, keeping things in the same place, and organizing
your notes will give you more free time in the end.

9. DO THE NASTIES. You will accumulate unpleas-
ant tasks and hassles that need to be handled but are
always at the bottom of the list. Take a few hours every
so often and knock them out. It feels so good.

10. SELF-CONFIDENCE IS KEY. People believe in
people who act with assurance. Leaders exude confidence without arrogance.

Mark had already employed numbers 1, 2, and 8 during our trip
together. He never turned down a challenging opportunity, he
was constantly in motion, and his backpack containing the "tools
of his trade" was highly (if unintentionally) organized. In truth,

Mark followed all the maxims on the list except, perhaps, number six. To my knowledge he had not been ballroom dancing.

As we walked, Mark conveyed what he'd read in anticipation of meeting George. Many Christian families moved from Bethlehem to nearby areas like Beit Sahour as Muslim refugees began settling in Bethlehem, and Beit Sahour's population is overwhelmingly Christian (we later learned that George is Greek Orthodox). During the First Intifada (the Palestinian uprising from 1987 to 1993 against the Israeli occupation), Beit Sahour made the international news when residents united in a nonviolent protest. In response to the lack of representation Palestinians had in Israeli government, Beit Sahour's citizens adopted the motto "no taxation without representation" and stopped paying the taxes levied on them by Israel. Israel reacted with military force. The Israeli military deemed the entire village a "closed military zone," imposed a strict curfew, cut telephone lines, ransacked homes and shops, arrested and detained people without charges, and prevented entrance by anyone, even Christian bishops attempting to bring in truckloads of food. When Yitzhak Rabin, then Israeli defense minister, told Israeli soldiers to "break the bones of Palestinians," Beit Sahour's families opened their homes to Jewish Israelis, inviting them to "break bread, not bones." Many Jewish families accepted the open invitation and made their way to Beit Sahour, where they spent Shabbat, the Jewish holy day, with Palestinian host families.

Continuing our walk, I realized the truth in Rex's first two pieces of advice to Mark. I had arrived with some deep concerns about traveling in areas under Palestinian control, but at least so far, I discovered my concern was unwarranted. Beit Sahour wasn't at all what I had expected. It was a middle-class village. Nearly all the residents and workers we passed wore Western dress. Teens and children wore jeans and tee shirts, even the girls. Though we saw no other American tourists, I didn't sense that we appeared out of place. Though not exactly expecting furtive glances from glowering tribesmen, I was surprised at the overt friendliness of some and the calm indifference of others.

The Siraj Center was located in an old building at the corner of a busy intersection, and we found George's office on the second floor. George, handsome and muscular with an engaging smile, was on the telephone, but he quickly ended the call when we appeared at his door. He stood up and warmly greeted us with handshakes and hearty hugs. His office was small but comfortable, with the rumbling sounds of diesel-powered trucks and the blaring horns of impatient taxis pouring through the open windows. Over the roaring din, he introduced us to two others in his office, Hisham and Tamer, both Palestinian tour guides. A group of students, most college-age, worked in second-floor offices near George's, and from time to time, one opened the door to George's office to ask for his opinion about something or other. I was fascinated by all the activity in this compact space. George explained that they were in the middle of the Siraj Center's annual summer program for international students and handed Mark a flyer about the program, "Come and Celebrate Palestine." Students in the program stayed with Palestinian families, studied Palestinian history and Arabic, toured historical and holy sites, and worked on service projects and cultural activities.

George's office overflowed with street noises, sounds of scraping chairs, and voices of young people working in adjoining spaces. In the midst of the commotion, George was remarkably calm and engaging. He told us about the Siraj Center, its goal of sharing Palestinian history and culture with people around the world, and its many programs and activities. The Siraj Center offered a selection of multi-day guided nature walks, including an eleven-day walk along the route Joseph and Mary took from Nazareth to Bethlehem, with hikers staying with Palestinian families each evening. It also had various activities to introduce participants to the Palestinian/Israeli conflict, including conferences with Palestinian and Israeli government officials and peace groups, tours of areas of conflict, and meetings with people who are directly affected by the Israeli occupation. One of the goals, George said, was to strengthen the Palestinian economy by developing more international tourism.

"But Israel's policies are making it almost impossible for Palestinians to develop tourism," George said as he swiveled his chair to face the window. "In many ways, Israel has wiped historic Palestine off the map, and the area is coming to be known as Israel."

George explained that Israel's tourism office failed to differentiate between Israel and the West Bank. Its official maps of "Israel" included the lands in both Israel and the Palestinian territories, but showed no borders. (As he spoke, I recalled my confusion when Mark and I drove from Ein Gedi to the West Bank's Jordan Valley, and I couldn't find the Israel-West Bank border on the map.) Israeli tour operators were permitted to work throughout Israel and the West Bank, but Palestinian operators were prohibited from working in Israel or Israeli-controlled areas in the West Bank, about 90 percent of the land of historic Palestine. Israel controlled access to some of the most important historic, archaeological, and religious sites of historic Palestine. Jerusalem, the very heart of historic Palestine, had been usurped by Israel, surrounded by checkpoints, and cut off by the Separation Wall.

Mark shared our experience earlier that day about having to locate the Arab bus station in Jerusalem and about our uncomfortable crossing through the Israeli checkpoint. Then, pulling a notebook and pen out of his daypack, he asked about other ways the Israeli occupation has affected West Bank's residents and visitors. Mark was all business when it came to taking notes.

At the outset, George said he preferred "Palestinian" to "Arab" when speaking of the Palestinian people. "Arab," he said, was a vague, amorphous term referring to a group of Arab states, and using it to describe Palestinians wrongly associated all Palestinians with political Islam and pan-Arabism, and blurred the distinction between the humanitarian crisis in Palestine and the larger conflict between Israel and other Arab countries.

"Of course, all people who live in the West Bank are affected by the occupation, as are people who travel here," George said, referring to Mark's question.

"Israel controls travel to, from, and within the West Bank," he pointed out. He went on to explain that Israel controls the air space, and Palestinians are prohibited from building or operating an airport. Travelers bound for the West Bank can fly into the Israeli airport, arrive by ship at an Israeli port, or cross the border from a neighboring country, but whether they arrived by air, sea, or land, they are required to pass through one or more Israeli checkpoints—and Israel controls who passes through those checkpoints. George said that even Palestinians living in other countries have been refused entry into the West Bank. He explained that, since the beginning of the occupation in 1967, Israel has required West Bank Palestinians be registered with the Israeli government, and only registered Palestinians are eligible for an Israeli-issued identification card. Palestinians from other countries, however, are not eligible to register. Palestinians from other countries who want to be reunited with family members in the West Bank must apply with the Israeli government for family reunification, and Israel has frozen all family-reunification requests since the Second Intifada.

George told us the story of one Palestinian family's frustrating attempt to reunite. There were two brothers, one who lived in the West Bank and the other in Jordan. The one in the West Bank applied for a building permit from the Israeli government to build a home on his family's land. About the same time, the brother in Jordan applied for an entry pass from the Israeli government so he could live with his brother in the West Bank. Israel denied the building permit application of the first brother due to insufficient proof of land ownership, even though he presented a deed and tax records dating back to the Ottoman era. (George explained that Israel has frozen land registration in the West Bank for the past thirty years, so that no land can be registered in the name of a Palestinian; in order to obtain a building permit, Palestinians are required to prove ownership dating back before the Israeli occupation, and Israel routinely judges any documentation presented as insufficient.) Israel also denied the other brother's application for an entry pass into the West Bank from Jordan—he was not registered with the Israeli government, and Israeli officials refused to consider his family unification request. At this point, the brother in the West Bank gave up his dreams of building a house and decided to relocate to Jordan. He packed up his belongings and set out for the King Hussein Bridge, where Israeli soldiers stopped him and refused to let him cross the bridge into Jordan for "security reasons," though they would not explain the "security reasons." He returned to his village in the West Bank, where he waited several months for approval from the Israeli government to leave for Jordan.

George continued his descriptions of other hurdles Palestinians face under the Israeli occupation. In the West Bank, travel for residents and tourists alike is often disrupted by the hundreds of Israeli roadblocks on Palestinian roads. Israeli-constructed roadblocks funnel Palestinian traffic to Israeli checkpoints, where soldiers stop and search cars and trucks. A search can last several hours or an entire day, and drivers' schedules are completely dependent on the whim of the Israeli security forces manning the roadblock. Serious, reliable business could not truly take place without a guarantee of unobstructed travel. These disruptions have hobbled Palestinian tourism, strangled the larger Palestinian economy, and made life tense and unpredictable for the Palestinian people. Israel claims the roadblocks are necessary for security reasons, despite the fact that most of the roadblocks are on Palestinian roads between Palestinian communities nowhere near the Israeli border.

George moved on to one of the most persistent issues in the Palestinian territories—access to potable water. "Many Palestinians live from day to day not knowing whether they will have water. How can you operate a hotel or business or school or hospital if you don't have water?" For those Palestinian communities connected to network water service, supply varies drastically, with some areas having daily service and others receiving water every month or two. Even in areas that generally have daily service, like Bethlehem, water can be completely cut off without prior notice or explanation. Last summer, a severe drought left Bethlehem with no running water for a month. The unpredictable water supply has forced many Palestinians to build water tanks, which they fill when water was available. "You can tell the difference between the Palestinian villages and the Israeli settlements in the West Bank," George said, "because most Palestinian houses feature water tanks on top and the settlers' houses don't. There is always running water in the Israeli settlements."

Despite the West Bank's abundant natural water resources, Palestinians are suffering from what George called "a man-made drought" because Israel severely restricts Palestinian access to water. Before the Israeli occupation, Palestinians relied on surface water from the Jordan River and groundwater from aquifers underlying the West Bank. After the occupation began 1967, Israel took control of all water resources and infrastructure, abrogated Palestinian water rights, destroyed all Palestinian pumps along the Jordan River, and prohibited Palestinians from using water without Israeli approval. In 1995, the Oslo Accords established a Joint Water Committee to manage West Bank aquifer water and projects (the Jordan River waters were not included and continue to be totally off-limits to Palestinians). The problem is that Israel was given exclusive veto power over all Palestinian water projects, and has used this power to deny Palestinians access to their rightful share of water and to severely restrict Palestinian infrastructure projects. Approximately one-third of Palestinian communities are not even connected to a water network. Many communities rely on water delivered by tankers, with some communities surviving on as little as twelve liters of water (of questionable quality) per person a day. Meanwhile, Israel routinely over-extracts its share of water from West Bank aquifers, often by as much as 50 percent, and has constructed a network of large high-pressure pipelines to serve the Jewish settlers in the West Bank. Those 450,000 Jewish settlers together use more water than all 2.3 million Palestinians in the West Bank. Last summer, during Bethlehem's month without water, Israeli settlements doubled their water usage and settlers enjoyed lush lawns and full swimming pools. At this point, I thought about my green lawn and pristine pool back in Austin. Mark later admitted that he had, too.

In the part of the West Bank located in Area C (about 60 percent of the West Bank), where many Palestinians are not connected to a water network, Israel routinely denies Palestinian requests for drilling new wells. Israel has even denied Palestinian requests for approval to repair old wells to make them operational and requests for approval to construct cisterns to collect rainwater. "Israel is using water as a tool of harassment, as a tool of displacement," George concluded, "making your life so miserable that you want to leave."

Mark had been taking rapid notes throughout our visit, but now his hand lay still over his notebook as he listened. Water was an issue in Texas, but never like this. It was inconceivable to us that water would be used as a weapon.

While speaking of the myriad of obstacles presented by the Israeli occupation, George seemed optimistic about the possibility of changing things for the better. But from time to time he would abruptly stop talking, and a disheartened expression would cross his face. At one point, perhaps overwhelmed by the grim reality of the situation, he reflected, "There's a gradual wearing down of Palestinians through building permits, identification cards, checkpoints, water . . . everything."

George paused and glanced at his watch. I realized we had taken most of his afternoon, and Mark still had an impressive list to investigate and write about. Before leaving George's office, Hisham offered to take us to Hebron the following day, and Mark, who had to cover the city for Let's Go, enthusiastically accepted his offer. Seeing Hebron in the company of an insider and new friend would give Mark an edge in writing reviews for his publication. We bid farewell to George and left Siraj Center. Departing Beit Sahour, I noticed a building painted celadon, one side of which was adorned with a stencil of an angel with crimson hearts falling from her fingers. The hearts appeared to scatter over a heap of broken concrete and rusted iron on the sidewalk. Everywhere we looked, so much beauty lay within so much brokenness.

That night in the Old City of Jerusalem, Mark and I stayed late at Yerevan, a pizza restaurant and hookah parlor in the Christian Quarter, which had been highly recommended by Yousef.

The tiny restaurant was paneled in dark wood and glass and decorated with artificial garlands and a Christmas tree. A television was tuned to Arabic music videos. While we waited for our pizza, we never mentioned Yerevan's unique décor. We talked instead about the "man-made drought" in the West Bank caused by Israel's control over the water. "Oslo was supposed to be a temporary arrangement—to remain in place until Israelis and Palestinians reached a permanent peace agreement," Mark said. "But what incentive does Israel have to negotiate with the Palestinians when, by just maintaining the status quo, Israel can continue to control all the water?" I could feel myself becoming anxious as Mark talked. Water certainly seemed to be a major problem in the West Bank, but what about the other problems George told us about—the Israeli roadblocks and checkpoints that hobbled daily life and the economy, the Israeli restrictions on Palestinian travel, the Israeli prohibitions on Palestinian land registration, the Israeli denial of Palestinian building permits? But Mark's mood quickly lightened. It had been some time since he'd had pizza, and he was thrilled to see and smell our order coming out of the kitchen. After we finished the entire pizza, our waiter delivered a *nargileh* pipe (a Turkish water pipe used for smoking flavored tobacco). Neither Mark nor I were regular smokers, but we always tried local customs when traveling and had experienced hookah a few years back while on a family vacation in East Berlin. The waiter set the tall pipe on the floor near our table and lit the tobacco. Mark, who had his hair pulled straight back into a ponytail, dark curls shooting out behind him, drew smoke from the slender tube of the pipe and practiced timing smoke rings to the shifting beat of the Arabic music, which prompted a lot of laughter followed by a ring-blowing contest with three middle-aged men sitting at a table nearby. This singular activity kept us at the restaurant until most places in Old City were shuttered for the night. When we finally headed back to the guesthouse, the narrow, winding streets were pitch dark and nearly deserted. It was Shabbat, a day of rest for observant Jews, which begins at sundown on Friday and ends at sundown on Saturday. We walked, laughing about the smoke rings and the very entertaining men who'd made it a game.

Back at the Lutheran Guesthouse, I emailed Rex, attaching a photograph I'd taken on my phone of Mark blowing smoke rings. Later, I received an email from Rex. He and Paul were in Thackerville, Oklahoma, where they were playing poker at WinStar, a casino owned and operated by the Chickasaw Nation. "We're such great parents. You're smoking shisha with one son, and I'm at a casino gambling with the other. We would be excommunicated from the Northside Church of Christ for sure."

Closed Military Zones and Flying Checkpoints

Saturday, July 4, morning.

What was it about politics and the month of July? The French celebrated Bastille Day. Mark and I "celebrated" our own country's Independence Day very differently, but fittingly, this year in Hebron, one of the most contentious cities in the West Bank. Before planning this trip, I had barely been aware of the existence of Hebron. But since arriving in Israel, it had regularly slipped on and off Mark's computer screen. Hebron was the only Palestinian city with Jewish settlements right in the center, and there was a long history of violence between the Jewish settlers and the Palestinian Muslims who made up most of the city's population. I am sure, had I asked any stranger on the streets of Jerusalem or in the gardens of Ein Gedi Kibbutz, they would have resoundingly warned me against traveling there. Yet there I was loading my oversized purse with items I might find handy in that pocket of ongoing violence.

Mark and I arranged to meet Hisham, the Palestinian guide George had introduced us to the day before, in Beit Ummar, a village on the northern outskirts of Hebron. From the Lutheran

Guesthouse, we threaded a path through the masses of Saturday morning shoppers in the Old City's *souq* (Arab marketplace) and gently edged through the crowds congregating on the vast stone courtyard outside Damascus Gate. Festively colored umbrellas stood shading cartons of shoes, handbags, sunglasses, scarves, and relatively modest ladies' lingerie. We walked along the heavily trafficked Sultan Suleyman Street to the Arab bus station (as it is known in all the travel guides, though George would prefer "Palestinian" bus station) and boarded a bus to the Israeli checkpoint. Once again we filed through the checkpoint building on foot and, after passing inspection by Israeli soldiers, exited the other side to find a Palestinian taxi driver. A week ago, I felt just this side of hysterical over the idea of crossing into Palestinian-controlled areas. Just a day ago, my heart rate elevated sliding into a Palestinian-operated taxi. Those concerns had been put to rest after visiting Bethlehem and Beit Sahour and meeting the people in George's office. Today's destination, however, held a legitimate cause for concern.

While in the taxi on the way to Beit Ummar, Mark's cell phone rang. It was Hisham calling to say he would be delayed. After a brief conversation, with Mark's contribution being a few "okays" and raised eyebrows, Mark filled me in. "Remember the news about the volunteers going to the Safa farm to protect the Palestinian farmers from the Jewish settlers? Last Saturday, Israeli soldiers blocked volunteers from entering the farm. Hisham has to go interview someone who was injured." Mark and I had both read the news about the Safa farmers while at Ein Gedi Kibbutz. The Palestinian farmers were being threatened by a group of aggressive stone-throwing Jewish settlers. The settlers' apparent goal was to prevent the farmers from harvesting their grape orchards so they could claim the land had not been farmed and take it to expand their settlement. Volunteers gathered at Safa every Saturday morning in an attempt to prevent the settlers from attacking the farmers. Mark reflected momentarily on the situation—and perhaps also on those familiar maxims "when in doubt, go for it" and "action is better than inaction"—and then suggested (no, insisted) we go help the Safa farmers. "It sure beats standing here waiting for Hisham." I am not sure now why I agreed so readily to throw myself between rock-throwing Jewish settlers and Palestinian farmers, but I think I was swept up in the emotion in Mark's voice.

Our cab driver had lived in Palestine his entire life but had never been to the village of Khirbet Safa. He maneuvered his battered taxi through the terraced slopes and hillside villages, dodging women in hijabs and men in *taqiyah* (caps worn by Muslim men) who appeared out of nowhere here and there on roadside footpaths. Our driver made frequent, lurching stops that made my stomach churn in order to ask directions from startled pedestrians.

Nearing the Safa farm, a band of green-black military jeeps and tanks formed a wall blocking the road. An Israeli soldier bounded from one of the jeeps toward the taxi, shouting at us to get out. I caught a glimpse of our driver's worried expression in the rearview mirror as I opened the car door. Outside the taxi, Mark explained to the soldier that we were tourists, and as requested, we handed over our passports. I looked over at Mark, repressing a surge of panic as I remembered that Israeli Defense Forces could detain and deport political activists without an explanation. Even I had to admit that Mark looked subversive. Black stubble bristled from his cheeks and chin. Belligerent curls sprung from his unmanageable head of hair. Stale shisha and pizza aromas emanated from his rumpled tee shirt and worn hiking pants. Stashed in his backpack were the notes he'd taken at George's office about the endless ways Israel was stifling Palestinian tourism and making life unbearable for tourists and Palestinians alike. What if the soldiers took him away? What if they took us both away? I looked down at the black stretchy skirt I'd worn and slept in for nearly two weeks and at my blue flip-flops. While this time regretting my decision to scrape the tiny Israeli flags off the flip-flops, I was pretty sure I looked more like a tourist than a political activist.

I was impressed by how cool-headed Mark remained, considering his apparent anger just moments ago. Meanwhile, we stood frozen in place while the soldier huddled with other uniformed and armed guards near the blockade. (My teeth were so tightly clenched during the encounter that my jaw was mildly sore for the rest of the day.) After passing around and inspecting our passports, there was some muffled conversation followed by a few walkie-talkie calls. Then the soldier returned, informing us that no one was permitted to enter the Safa farm. The IDF had deemed it a "closed military zone."

Once safe in the taxi, my relief was mixed with curiosity and a flood of frustration. If the Safa farmers needed the protection of volunteers in order to harvest their land, then it was likely no harvest would take place that day. If the farmers stopped harvesting their land, they risked losing it to the Jewish settlers. Was the IDF helping the Jewish settlers by declaring the Safa farm a "closed military zone"? Our good-natured cab driver appeared more relieved than curious. As a Palestinian attempting to cross an Israeli blockade, he was the most likely of the three of us to be arrested and taken into custody by the IDF.

Did we simply imagine that our cab driver seemed in a rush to drop us off at a gas station in Beit Ummar and drive away? Now on our own, we waited for Hisham, aware that we were a novelty in this tiny village that straddled the main road to Hebron. On the side of the road where we stood near the gas station, there was a tiny convenience store that sold cigarettes and telephone calling cards; on the other side of the road was a fruit stand filled with baskets overflowing with peaches. Several young Palestinian men dressed in tee shirts and jeans congregated in front of the convenience store, smoking cigarettes and talking. They smiled and nodded, and we smiled and nodded back.

Moments later another cab drove up. A young and very attractive blonde in the back seat rolled down the window and asked in a German accent, "Do you know how to get to the Safa farm?" I took this as evidence that a significant number of international volunteers were coming to the aid of the Safa farmers in order to keep the settlers from disrupting the harvest—and that a significant number of Palestinian cab drivers had no clue how to get to Khirbet Safa.

Mark described our recent experience with the IDF blockade at the Safa farm and, after chatting with her for a few minutes, suggested she join us on the tour of Hebron. It took her less than a heartbeat to sign on to our plan.

As it turned out, the young woman, whose name was Jana, had previous experience with nonviolent resistance activities in support of Palestinians. She had joined the residents of Bil'in in one of their weekly Friday afternoon demonstrations in front of the "work-site of shame." At that site, Israeli forces were constructing the Israeli Separation Wall through the middle of Bil'in's agricultural land on the Palestinian side of the Green Line. As she and Mark talked about the situation in Bil'in, I sensed that a Friday afternoon visit to Bil'in was in Mark's future. That would take care of the first two items on Rex's list. (It wasn't until later that I recalled what I'd read about Israeli soldiers shooting high-powered tear-gas cannons into the crowd at one of the weekly protests in Bil'in.)

Now, with Jana standing next to us, the Palestinian men moved closer. The presence of the European blonde, who spoke both English and Arabic in addition to her native German, appeared to make the men extremely animated and talkative. In no time at all, one of the men approached her: "Where are you from?" "What are you doing in Palestine?" "Are you married?" After Jana responded "no" to his last question, he darted across the street to his peach stand and returned with three plump, ripe peaches, the first of which he offered to Jana.

Minutes later, Hisham pulled up, unknowingly rescuing Jana from her Palestinian suitor. He stepped out of his small black sedan, wearing a short-sleeved blue and white checked button-down shirt that was tucked neatly into his black trousers, and greeted us in his customary warm manner. Hisham, we learned, had spent many years working as a newscaster, and this was obvious from his demeanor. During the time we spent with him, he consistently looked us directly in the eyes while talking, rarely blinked, never fidgeted, and always smiled. His smile grew especially big when Mark told him that Jana would be joining us for the day.

As we piled in the car, Hisham apologized for his tardiness. He said he was delayed by a "flying checkpoint." When we told him we'd never heard of "flying checkpoints" (I envisioned something out of *Wicked*), he explained that a flying checkpoint was a temporary IDF checkpoint where the Israeli military stationed tanks on either side of a road, stopped all traffic, and inspected cars. "The IDF sets up flying checkpoints on Palestinian roads all the time, even though they already have hundreds of permanent checkpoints and roadblocks," said Hisham. "But when Israel releases to news agencies the number of checkpoints it has in the West Bank, in an effort to show how Israel is easing up on Palestinian movement restrictions, it does not include the flying checkpoints."

Due to the delay, Hisham had not yet interviewed the Palestinian man who was injured by Israeli soldiers at the Safa farm last Saturday. He would have to take us with him to the meeting, and afterward, he would take us to Hebron.

A short, bumpy distance from Beit Ummar, Hisham slowed the car to a stop in front of a small, ranch-style house. A woman named Beckah, who appeared to be in her late twenties, welcomed us and pointed Hisham to the interview room. Meanwhile, Mark,

Jana, and I joined Beckah in the living room, where several international volunteers sat on cushions on the floor, working on laptops. Beckah, despite her relative youth, had a commanding presence, enhanced no doubt by her vividly red, waist-length hair. While serving tea, she told us that she was American, her father Jewish, and her boyfriend Palestinian, and that she had spent the last several years helping Palestinian farmers.

Beckah talked for nearly an hour about the Safa farm and Bat Ayin, the Israeli settlement on the hilltop overlooking the farm. The Bat Ayin settlers were trying to prevent the Safa farmers from harvesting the land because, as we'd heard earlier, the settlers wanted to take it. Settlers repeatedly attacked the farmers, usually pelting them with rocks, and had started fires to destroy the farmers' trees. Because of the violence, volunteers began going to the farm to protect the farmers while they harvested their grape orchards. The presence of volunteers with cell phones and video cameras generally kept the settlers at bay. Two weeks before, the settlers from Bat Ayin staged a nighttime attack and set fire to the Safa farm, burning more than a hundred fruit trees. The following morning, when farmers and volunteers arrived for the harvest, they were told the area was a "closed military zone." And just last week, volunteers accompanying farmers to the harvest site were stopped by IDF soldiers, who beat several of them and arrested twenty-six. If confronted, how far would I go to protect a Palestinian farmer? I didn't have to ask myself about Mark. It was clear by now he'd committed "the list" to heart.

Beckah pointed out that the Israeli military's action in declaring the Safa farm a "closed military zone" was illegal: a recent ruling by the Israeli High Court of Justice prevented the military from declaring an area a "closed military zone" in order to keep farmers from their land. "If the Safa farmers don't work their land, the Israeli government can consider the land abandoned, confiscate it, and use it to expand the Bat Ayin settlement." Beckah's tone grew more strident. "This is the pattern in the West Bank. The Israeli military obstructs access to land so Palestinians can't use it and then declares it abandoned and takes it to expand Israeli settlements." (I later read a United Nations report confirming that Israel had, in fact, requisitioned for Israeli settlements Palestinian land deemed by the Israeli military to be abandoned, including land that was abandoned only because the Israeli military had deemed it a "closed military zone.")

The Israeli settlements, Beckah argued, are illegal because Israel is occupying the West Bank as a result of the 1967 war, and international law prohibits a country from moving its civilians into a country it occupies as a result of war. Yet the Israeli government continues to disregard international law and enables and encourages settlement of the West Bank. Despite all of my legal training in handling disputes and disruptions, I was not prepared for this overwhelming rush of facts or the emotional response they provoked. It was clear that Beckah could have talked for hours about the injustices she had witnessed in the West Bank, and I could have listened. But Hisham appeared at the doorway, announcing with a smile, "Let's go."

Stink Water and Nasty Graffiti

Saturday, July 4, afternoon.

From Beit Ummar, Jana and I bounced and jostled in the back seat of Hisham's car as he navigated the uneven roads through the Judaean Hills toward Hebron. In the front passenger seat, Mark, with his athlete's sense of balance, absorbed the road shock rather gracefully. It was a talent he'd honed skateboarding in Austin's hills and balancing on sheer rock faces. During the short, seven-mile drive, Hisham, a native Hebronite, briefed us on the recent history and political landscape of the city. Hebron was the largest city in the West Bank, home to 190,000 Palestinians, many of whom had fled or were forced out of their home villages in Israeli territory in 1948. For the Muslims who made up a majority of the population, Hebron was venerated as one of the holy cities of Islam. It was the site of the tomb of the patriarch Abraham and the Ibrahimi Mosque, a two-thousand-year-old shrine in Hebron's Old City believed to be the burial place of the biblical couples Abraham and Sarah, Isaac and Rebecca, and Jacob and Leah. The shrine was sacred not only to Muslims but to Christians and Jews as well. (I wondered whether the young Israeli checkpoint guards, cool and anonymous behind their dark glasses, remembered that they shared religious ancestors with their Palestinian neighbors.) Following the Israeli occupation, some of the most religiously and politically extreme of ultra-Orthodox Jews settled in the heart of Hebron, in close proximity to the Ibrahimi Mosque, known to Jews as the Cave of Machpela.

We entered Hebron at Ras al Jora, the city's northern entrance, which took us along a thoroughfare divided by a palm-lined esplanade and bordered by flat-roofed buildings, newsstands, drug stores, hardware stores, restaurants, and Internet cafés. On the roadsides, boys in tee shirts and jeans rode bicycles, and women walked together, the older ones in hijabs and long dresses and the younger ones in hijabs and jeans. Hisham pointed to a billboard announcing, "Welcome to Hebron, Home of Fatah." Before the Hebron City Council had it repainted, Hisham said with a sly smile, the sign read, "Welcome to Hebron, Home of Hamas." Jana recalled passing many signs in the West Bank that were, perhaps, a little cynical, though only someone aware of the Palestinian political situation would catch the irony. Changing "Hamas" to "Fatah" would not change people's views, and it was likely that many Hebronites remained supporters of Hamas, the Islamic militant group that won an overwhelming victory over Fatah in Hebron in the 2006 elections. I thought to myself that the change might have been a sensible survival maneuver—just the name "Hamas" sounded alarms in the United States and international press because it was considered by many to be a terrorist organization. Just days before it had set off my own alarm response. The Hebron City Council's actions were politically correct, because

Fatah was recognized internationally as the only legitimate representative of the Palestinian people.

As we neared the city center, Hisham explained that Hebron was the only Palestinian city not accorded self-rule as part of the Oslo peace process, due to the presence of the Jewish settlements in the city center. In 1994, in the midst of negotiations for control of the city, one of Hebron's ultra-Orthodox settlers Baruch Goldstein, did the unthinkable. Without provocation, he opened fire with an M-16 on Palestinian Muslims who were kneeling in prayer at the Ibrahimi Mosque, killing twenty-nine. (Goldstein belonged to the extremest Israeli political organization Kach, which advocated the forceful expulsion of Palestinians from the West Bank; after the Goldstein massacre, Israel banned Kach.) Following the massacre, Hamas abandoned its policy of attacking only Israeli military targets and began taking revenge on Israeli civilians with suicide bombings and attacks, bringing negotiations for control of Hebron to an abrupt stop. Finally, in 1997, Israel and the Palestinian Authority signed the Hebron Protocol, a temporary agreement that placed 80 percent of the city under Palestinian control, an area designated H-1. The remaining 20 percent remained under Israeli control in an area designated H-2. "Most Palestinians were upset over the agreement," Hisham said. "In addition to the Jewish settlements where four hundred fifty settlers lived, the H-2 Israeli-controlled area included the sacred Ibrahimi Mosque, the Old City Arab marketplace, and the homes of thirty-five thousand Palestinians." To provide security for the relatively small Jewish settlements, Israel staged a military buildup in the Israeli-controlled H-2 area of Hebron. "There are over one hundred Israeli roadblocks, rooftop monitoring towers, and checkpoints on the ground. There are five Israeli soldiers for every one settler." This was an abrupt revelation into what "occupation" meant for Hebron's Palestinian population.

Hisham pulled the car into a parking space in the city center, near the Israeli-controlled H-2 area. Mark, who sat in the front passenger seat rapidly taking notes for the Hebron section of *Let's Go*, glanced up in search of a street sign. Seeing none, he asked Hisham about the name. "It depends on whether you are Palestinian or Israeli," Hisham replied. Noting Mark's puzzled expression, he explained, "After the Israeli occupation, Israel changed many street names. Palestinians still call them by their names before occupation." The street we were on, Ein Sarah, eventually turned into a-Shuhada (Street of the Martyrs) in the older, now Israeli-controlled area of the city. Israelis, however, knew it as King David Street. Many of the secondary roads, it turned out, didn't even have official names and were known by the names of the Palestinian families whose homes lined the road. I was glad I hadn't make arrangements to rent a GPS device to use in the West Bank.

Before touring the marketplace, the Ibrahimi Mosque, and other landmarks and businesses that Mark would write about for *Let's Go*, Hisham took us to a Palestinian neighborhood, Tel Rumeida, located within the Israeli-controlled area of Hebron. He had arranged for us to have tea at the home of a Palestinian family, the Al-Azzehs.

The Palestinian neighborhood Tel Rumeida was hemmed in at the top and the bottom of the hill by Jewish settlements and surrounded by Israeli checkpoints, military stations, and rooftop monitoring towers—one right on top of a Palestinian home. Israeli forces maintained strict control over the movement of Tel Rumeida's Palestinian residents, who had to pass through Israeli checkpoints to get to their homes. Palestinians, prohibited from driving in their own neighborhood, had to walk on designated inferior secondary roads and dangerous footpaths. (The Jewish settlers had full access to well-maintained streets for both driving and walking.)

To get to the Al-Azzehs' house, Mark, Jana, and I followed Hisham up one of the few roads open to Palestinian pedestrians. Midway up the hill, Hisham stopped and pointed out a Jewish settlement at the top (the settlers call the settlement by the same name as the surrounding Palestinian neighborhood, Tel Rumeida). At the entrance of the settlement was an Israeli Defense Forces post, where two Israeli guards in green fatigues and red berets stood with assault rifles. On the road just beyond the IDF post, ultra-Orthodox Jewish adolescent boys with long peyot and colorful kippahs stood, yelling at us in Hebrew. A settler woman, in a long-sleeved blouse and an ankle-length skirt, stood at a doorway nearby, staring intently. The ultra-Orthodox kids hurled epithets at us and used handheld mirrors to reflect the sun's rays into our faces and eyes. I shielded my eyes from the assault with my forearm. I noticed that Hisham kept his eyes focused on the ground. This felt more sinister than a little boyish rock-throwing. What on earth were these children up to? "After Tel Rumeida's Palestinian residents started videotaping Jewish settlers who yelled at them and attacked them," Hisham replied, "the settlers taught their children how to blind unwanted visitors

who carried cameras." (When Hisham told us about the Palestinian residents videotaping interactions with Jewish settlers, he was
referring to video cameras the Israeli human rights organization
B'Tselem distributed to Palestinians living in Hebron and other
contentious areas in the West Bank. The cameras enable Palestinian families to record the hardships they endure daily under the
Israeli occupation, and B'Tselem posts the videos on its website to
educate Israelis and other viewers.)

Hisham herded us off the road to a rutted and rock-strewn
footpath that would take us to the back entrance of the Al-
Azzehs' property. The footpath provided the only means of access
to the property, which included their flat-roofed house and a small
olive grove. The Israeli forces designated the main street front-
ing the Al-Azzehs' house a "Jewish only" street, which the family was not allowed to use. Mark, Jana, and I followed Hisham
along the dirt path winding up the wooded hillside, helping each
other over huge boulders and other obstacles along the way. My
ankle twisted more than once. The blue flip-flops were definitely
not optimal footgear for this endeavor. On our way up the hill,
we passed a house almost completely covered with sturdy wire
mesh, resembling a cage for very large animals. Hisham explained
that many Palestinian families in the neighborhood screened their
homes to protect them from rock-throwing Jewish settlers.

When we reached the back entrance to the Al-Azzehs' house,
we could see the Jewish settlement's concrete compound yards
above us on the hill. "In 1984, Israeli settlers moved onto an
archaeological site at the top of that hill, where they lived in six
mobile homes," Hisham told us. "During the Second Intifada,

the settlers claimed the mobile homes were unsafe, and the Israeli government gave them permission to build a permanent structure to house the six families. But, instead of a six-family structure, the settlers built a compound to house sixteen families, and kept the mobile homes as well." Hisham added that the Jewish settlers who lived in the compound were among the most extreme in the West Bank. One was Baruk Marzel, who had been a member of the extremest group Kach. Hisham said he watched a video interview that took place in Marzel's office and saw a sign hanging on Marzel's wall: "I've already killed an Arab, and you?" (When I returned home, I watched the interview, which is part of a documentary called *Inside God's Bunker,* directed by Jewish filmmaker Micha X. Peled, and I saw for myself the "I've already killed an Arab, and you?" sign hanging on Marzel's wall.)

That last piece of information was sickening, but there was more. I was shocked to see the settlers' trash strewn between their hilltop compound and the Al-Azzehs' yard: glass bottles, tin cans, plastic containers, and rusted appliances—even an old washing machine, which, Hisham told us, almost hit Hasheem Al-Azzeh, who was working in his yard when the huge metal contraption came tumbling down the hill. I watched Mark survey the trash-strewn area just as he used to do outside our neighbors' homes on city-designated bulky-trash collection days, when he'd get up early to gather treasures before the trash trucks arrived. There were, however, no "treasures" here. His expression of anticipation shifted to one of disgust. The white wood gate that opened to the Al-Azzehs' house was spray-painted with graffiti, including a Star of David.

Nisreen Al-Azzeh had dark eyes and a full face framed by a black hijab patterned with rose, gray, and white flowers. She served us tea in her living room, where Hisham and Jana sat on the couch, knees pressed against the dark wood coffee table decorated with lace doilies and a basket of red flowers. Mark and I sat in matching brown upholstered chairs. With her youngest son in her lap and her other three children playing within hearing distance in a nearby room, Nisreen spoke with a soft voice, answering our many questions about daily life in Tel Rumeida as Hisham interpreted. She acknowledged the difficulty of having to take the dirt footpath to get to and from her home, carting groceries and other necessities up the rocky hillside. She said her husband, Hasheem, had to carry their youngest children up and down the steep path. When Hasheem's elderly father was sick, Hasheem and his brother carried him down the path to town to get a taxi. On another occasion, when Hasheem's father needed an ambulance, they were forced to call the International Red Cross because Palestinian ambulances were prohibited from entering Tel Rumeida. "But at least life now is better than the curfew," she said, referring to the round-the-clock curfew the Israeli military imposed on the Palestinians in the H-2 area during the Second Intifada. For more than three hundred seventy days, they could not leave their homes, except for brief periods when the curfew was lifted. She went on to describe the many inconveniences and humiliations suffered by her family during that time. One of the most horrifying incidents occurred when she was in labor with her youngest child. Hasheem helped her down the footpath to the Israeli checkpoint, but the Israeli guard would not allow them to pass through, telling her instead to "go die inside your home." The Al-Azzehs returned home, waited for a change in guard shifts, and then went back to the checkpoint, where a more sympathetic soldier let them through. Nisreen was fortunate that she made it to the hospital. (According to a United Nations report I later read, between September 2000 and June 2006, sixty-eight pregnant Palestinian women gave birth at Israeli checkpoints after being barred from crossing. Five of these women and thirty-five of the infants died.)

Nisreen said that the Jewish settlers wanted to make life unbearable for her family and the other Palestinians of Tel Rumeida. "They cut our water and phone lines, break our windows, ransack our homes, throw rocks at our children as they walk to school, and attack Hasheem when he harvests olives, saying the land belongs to them." Mark noted the similarity to the Safa farm situation and asked Nisreen how her family was countering the settlers' attacks and allegations. She explained that Hasheem had filed a lawsuit in Israeli court to keep the settlers from taking the land, and after five years, in 2006, the Israeli High Court of Justice ruled that the land belonged to the Al-Azzehs. But even after the court ruling, she said, the settlers continued to threaten Hasheem as he harvested olives—all while Israeli soldiers simply stood by. (When I returned to Austin, I discovered on YouTube a video of the Jewish settlers attempting to stop Hasheem Al-Azzeh from harvesting his olives.) Recently, settlers severed many of the Al-Azzehs' olive trees from their roots, a metaphor perhaps for what the settlers wanted to accomplish against all the Palestinian people of Hebron.

"The settlers want us to move off our land so they can have it," Nisreen said. "But this is our home. We have nowhere else to go. If we move, the settlers will take our land, then follow us to our new place and try to push us off so they can take that also."

Of the five hundred Palestinian families who once lived in Tel Rumeida, only fifty remained. "The Zionist leaders believe Palestine is a land without a nation that should be given to a nation without a land," Hisham told us. "In their view, we do not exist." As Hisham saw it, the main conflict, whether in Israel or in the Palestinian territories, concerned the land, and Israel's strategy was to make the lives of the Palestinian residents as difficult as possible in order to push them gradually off that land. "We believe the Israeli government is an instrument of legalizing the occupation. When there are exceptions—court rulings and other legal actions in favor of the Palestinian people, which is very infrequent—they will not be implemented."

Nisreen surprised me when she mentioned that she was an artist. With her four young children and arduous, time-consuming treks up and down the hillside to do her shopping and errands, I couldn't imagine how she found the time. But her recent works, skillfully rendered pastels on colored construction paper, were taped to the smooth white walls of the entryway of her home. One pictured a group of men and women holding up a "Free Palestine" banner and, in the background under a blue sky with a glowing yellow sun, the green hills of Hebron and the Israeli Separation Wall. Another portrayed a row of olive trees from the Al-Azzehs' grove, perfectly robust and thriving even though each was severed from its roots. Before departing, I offered Nisreen a few shekels for the pastel of the olive trees, which she accepted, and I slid her artwork between the travel documents in my over-sized purse. After saying our goodbyes and thanking Nisreen for her time and tea, Mark, Jana, and I followed Hisham back down the steep path to the secondary street, the one open to Palestinian pedestrians, where we once again were assailed from afar by the Jewish settlers' children.

Our route from Nisreen's house to the Old City marketplace took us around Beit Hadassah, the Jewish settlement near the bottom of the Tel Rumeida hillside. From our vantage point on a path just yards above the settlement, we watched as a caravan of settlers filed out of a synagogue following Saturday Shabbat services—the males, armed with rifles, leading the way. Hisham noted that the Israeli military allowed Jewish settlers to bear arms openly, while for Palestinians, simply owning a weapon could mean a lengthy prison stay, or worse. Once around Beit Hadassah, we continued down to the Old City marketplace. Mark, Jana, and I halted abruptly to gaze at the wire netting secured over the street to protect the few remaining Palestinian shop owners and customers from the Jewish settlers of Beit Hadassah. Above our heads, suspended in the net like gnats in an epically proportioned spider's web, were plastic bags, rotting food, barbed wire, rocks, hangers, bottles, and cans that settlers had lobbed down, targeting Palestinians. We stood, aghast, sickened by the sight and stench of the aerial garbage display. The street was sticky beneath our feet. "The settlers are very creative," Hisham told us. "Because most rocks and bottles won't pass through the net, the settlers fill plastic bags with urine or bleach. When the bags hit the wire, they pop and the stink water sprays all over the street." I could not take my eyes off the windows looming over our heads lest one of the bags of "stink water" set sail. On each side of the street, Israeli guards stood watching us from IDF monitoring towers with video surveillance cameras filming every move we made.

Just as they controlled Palestinians living in Tel Rumeida, Israeli forces maintained strict control over the movement of the Palestinians in other parts of Hebron's Israeli-controlled H-2 area. Hisham said that A-Shuhada Street, once the main shopping area in the Old City, was completely closed to Palestinians. The Israeli military padlocked the metal doors of the Palestinian shops that lined both sides of the street and gave Jewish settlers full use of the thoroughfare. The shop doors were covered with what Hisham referred to as "nasty graffiti"—hateful words scrawled in Hebrew by Jewish settlers. The hundreds of Palestinians living in the second-story apartments above their now-closed shops, were forced to climb through their windows and walk across rooftops to reach the parts of streets where they were allowed to walk. Balconies of Palestinian apartments overlooking a-Shuhada Street were encased in wire mesh, protection from rock-throwing Jewish settlers.

In the areas where Israel permitted Palestinian businesses to operate, the buildings and infrastructure were literally crumbling. Hisham told us that the Hebron Rehabilitation Committee, a semi-governmental organization, tried to improve the Old City area by repaving streets and improving services and infrastructure. "The HRC is trying to attract more Palestinian businesses to the area to replace those who left. But the settlers and IDF have highly successful strategies to counter the HRC's positive work: numerous checkpoints, road closures, video sur-veillance, and physical harassment of Palestinians." The IDF's strategies made it nearly impossible for Palestinian businesses to operate. The Israeli human rights organization B'Tselem esti-mated that these IDF strategies caused nearly 80 percent of the Palestinian businesses in H-2 to close. B'Tselem concluded that Israeli forces, in the process of protecting the Jewish settlers of Hebron, had caused the economic collapse of the entire city center.

Looking back, it seems impossible now that we could be hungry, after standing underneath rotting garbage and learning the depressing facts of Hebron life. But we were. And this time it was not just Mark; we were all famished. Apparently it took a great deal of energy to absorb so much bad news. We walked a few blocks to a square near the entrance to the Old City, where Hisham assured us we'd find a typical Palestinian restaurant. Once a prosperous commercial area, now most buildings were deteriorated and the shops shuttered. There were few people on the streets. Not surprisingly, we were the only tourists. One dilapidated building, which appeared to be partially bombed out, managed to escape having its metal doors sealed shut. Just outside its entrance, on one of the opened metal doors, someone had taped a sign with words printed by hand on orange con-struction paper:

FREEDOM COFFEE SHOP, HANTHALA
COFFEE, TEA, JUICES, SODA, ARGILEH,
WELCOME

Inside there were three tables of different sizes and a dozen or so mismatched chairs. The thick, crumbling concrete walls and dim light gave it the feel of a grotto. Because we were the only customers, Mark and Hisham dragged a couple of extra chairs to a table near a cooler displaying a sparse assortment of bottled drinks. At the far end, directly under a makeshift staircase of unfinished wood slats, was the "kitchen" area: one small table with an unplugged hotplate and several opened brown paper bags. While the owner, Muhammed, took containers of prepared foods out of the bags, I looked back at the Freedom Coffee Shop sign, which advertised no food items. Muhammed carefully divided the contents of the bags—flatbread, olives, shwarma, and hummus—into equal portions onto four paper plates and served us each a plate. Mark swallowed a scoop of hummus on flatbread, and then asked about the name on the sign, "Hanthala." Hisham explained it was the name of a cartoon character—a little refugee boy with tattered clothes and bare feet—drawn by the Palestinian cartoonist Naji Al-Aliwithwas. "Hanthala symbolizes the Palestinian struggle," said Hisham. I looked around. Still no other customers. This Palestinian neighborhood was a ghost town. Obviously, Muhammed was not making much money operating the Freedom Coffee Shop. Perhaps, like the Al-Azzehs, Muhammed remained in this place—a place now under Israeli occupation and labeled H-2, a place where Israeli soldiers and Jewish settlers alike were openly hostile to Palestinians—because his departure would amount to defeat, and he was not about to let the Israeli military or the Jewish settlers of Hebron win. Perhaps, like the Al-Azzehs, he was fighting the Israeli occupation with his simple presence.

Muhammed was Hanthala. He was a symbol of the Palestinian struggle. I looked over at Muhammed, who sat on the edge of a chair at a nearby table, legs crossed, smoking a cigarette and watching us eat. It occurred to me that he was probably thinking, *Wow! Customers!*

After lunch, Jana returned to Bethlehem to meet a group of friends and fellow activists. She assured us her Arabic was adequate enough to interpret schedules and find a bus that would take her there. She and Mark agreed to talk in the next day or so. After our time in Hebron, I felt certain that Mark, given the opportunity, would join her at the "work-site of shame" in Bil'in to protest the Israeli Separation Wall. Mark and I then walked a few blocks with Hisham to the Ibrahimi Mosque, which in the years following the Goldstein massacre had been permanently partitioned by the Israeli government into Muslim and Jewish sections, each with its own entrance. At the Muslim entrance were hijabs for female tourists like me; at the Jewish entrance was a gun check for armed Jewish settlers. After touring the mosque, we walked to perhaps the only Palestinian-owned guesthouse in the midst of the Israeli-controlled area, which was positioned in direct view of an Israeli guard station. At the guesthouse, appropriately named "Hanthala," Hisham introduced us to one of the guests, an Italian peace activist and filmmaker. Back in the car, Hisham took us to several places Mark wanted to review for *Let's Go*, including one of the glass-blowing plants for which Hebron is known, the Al Salam Glass and Pottery Factory, owned by the great-grandson of the Turk who brought the art to Palestine more than three hundred years ago.

It was late afternoon, dusk not far off, but the sun was still glaring and the heat oppressive. By this time we all were experiencing a tremendous conflict. We agreed that we hated to leave Hebron and, at the same time, we could not wait to get back to somewhere less tense, less dangerous. I, for one, was completely exhausted. We thanked Hisham, exchanging many hugs and handshakes and promises to keep in touch, and then boarded the bus that would take us to the Israeli checkpoint, and from there, Jerusalem.

During the trip to the checkpoint, Mark and I both began to feel extremely ill and dizzy, suffering from stomach cramps and the hot-cold chills of nausea. It seemed implausible that it was from our quick meal at Freedom Coffee Shop. Looking back at the day, especially our time lingering beneath the Jewish settlers' putrid garbage that was suspended above our heads in the nets and our distress upon hearing Nisreen's story about being turned back from the checkpoint while in labor, it was totally possible that we'd been poisoned by stress, sadness, and outrage.

Shabbat Desecraters Must Die!

Sunday, July 5.

During the course of a fitful night's sleep, the intermittent rumbling beyond the guesthouse's walls manifested itself in my dreams. I dreamed that I was with Rex in Austin, among the thousands packing the downtown riverfront for the annual Fourth of July symphony concert and fireworks display. In addition to the anniversary of our nation's birth, the event marked the anniversary of our first date. My sleep-fogged dreams then moved to the two of us staking out a spot near the river, spreading our blanket, and after the fusillade of cannon fire at the conclusion of Tchaikovsky's "1812 Overture," lying on our backs and reveling in the pyrotechnics display. I visualized soaring rockets bursting into brilliant star clusters and glittering weeping willows. The familiar and pleasant sounds of fireworks and applause suddenly shifted into a cacophony of explosions and screams. I remembered then that I was in Jerusalem, the site of dozens of Palestinian militant suicide attacks. Feverish and drained, I struggled to hear and understand the chaos and hysteria that echoed through the walls into our room, certain there had been a suicide bombing. I willed myself to get up and look out the window, but my body did not respond to the command. I was too weak to lift my head off the pillow. I drifted back to sleep.

In the full light of morning, I managed to roll over and bring the bed next to mine into focus. Mark slept on his stomach among a rumpled mass of sheets, blankets, and pillows, his head turned toward me, his mouth open. This was not the same young man who'd led me confidently into Hebron. On the bedside table, near a limp hand hanging over the edge of his bed, was a half-full bottle of Pepto-Bismal. I recalled how Mark and I boarded the bus in Hebron the afternoon before, each so ill we sat by open windows just in case, and how the bus was stopped at the Israeli checkpoint, where we were herded off with all the other passengers—Palestinians and internationals—seeking authorization to pass through, and how a teenaged Israeli soldier with long black hair and designer sunglasses separated me from Mark and separately questioned us about how we knew each other and what we had been doing in the West Bank. I recalled that I was so ill I could barely stand while she questioned me and I started crying. But I couldn't remember much about what had happened from that point on. Somehow Mark and I had made our way back to the guesthouse in Jerusalem and flopped onto our respective beds fully clothed.

Still in bed, I thought of the explosions that had made their way into my dreams. Or had they been more than a dream? Had there been a suicide bombing? This time I forced myself up and out of my own tangled covers, keeping my head tilted down to avoid feeling light-headed, and smoothed out my stretchy black outfit. I felt around the floor with my feet for my blue flip-flops with the Israeli flags partially scraped off, retrieving them with my toes and then padding silently to look out the window of our room. The guesthouse gardens were peaceful and undisturbed.

I tiptoed out of the room through the corridor to the guest-house lobby. I found Yousef working the morning shift at the front desk and questioned him about the commotion the night before. He appeared almost embarrassed as he told me there had been another violent protest outside the Jaffa gate because of the mayor's decision to open a parking lot in the Old City on Saturdays. He explained that the ultra-Orthodox Jews considered the mayor's decision to be official support for driving on Saturday, the Jewish holy day Shab-bat, when traditional Jewish law prohibits operating any type of machinery. They were not satisfied by the concessions the mayor offered to the ultra-Orthodox community, such as promising that the lot would be staffed by non-Jews and waiving parking fees so that no money would change hands, another Shabbat prohibition.

During Yousef's explanation, I glanced down at his desk and saw a copy of the Sunday edition of the *Jerusalem Post*, an English language newspaper. The front page pictured Israeli policemen drag-ging a Haredi man off the streets and an article about the parking lot incident:

HAREDI PROTESTERS: SHABBAT
DESECRATERS MUST DIE!
Masses of haredim [ultra-Orthodox Jews] demonstrated
and hurled rocks at police in Jerusalem on Saturday in
an ongoing protest against the opening of a parking
lot on Shabbat to accommodate weekend visitors to

the Old City. The protesters chanted that anyone who desecrates Shabbat "must die." To police seeking to rein them in, they warned, "You will burn in the fire of hell!" . . . [S]everal hundred haredim, yelling "Shabbos, Shabbos," "Nazis" and "anti-Semites" tried to break into the parking lot opposite the Jaffa Gate, but were forcibly prevented from entering the area by police.

The article went on to report that once Shabbat ended after sundown, a gang of protestors in an ultra-Orthodox neighborhood near the Old City employed the cover of darkness to set trashcans on fire, which caused explosions heard throughout the city. Israeli fireworks!

Reading further, I found a comforting voice of reason in one of the letters to the editor: "I am a Sabbath-observant, but believe everyone has the right to live as he or she wishes. If the haredim wish to be very, very strict in their observance of Shabbat, they should be at home with their families or in study groups learning Talmud, and not roaming the streets looking for, and causing, trouble and injury."

I thought of the exploding trashcans and of the angry ultra-Orthodox protestors calling the Israeli police "Nazis." Zamir came to mind. "They are nuts," he'd said jokingly. In this moment it seemed as though that were true.

Refugee Rappers

Following a quiet day of recovery and reading inside the tranquil rooms of the Lutheran Guesthouse in Jerusalem's Old City, we returned to several Palestinian-controlled areas in the West Bank. The first destination on Mark's *Let's Go* itinerary was the Dheisheh Refugee Camp. When Mark mentioned the camp, I was ambivalent. I imagined tents, squalor, and famine. Mark was charged with gathering information useful to travelers, but I wondered who would want to know the price of a room at a refugee camp. All the same, thanks to the editors at *Let's Go*, I had experienced some enlightening and enjoyable moments while accompanying Mark. Hebron had been harrowing at times, but I was extremely glad I had gone. So I packed my large black travel purse for the day's adventure and resolved to remain open to whatever the trip would bring. My understanding of the Palestinian situation was, after all, continually evolving.

We met up with Tamer, our guide for the day, on the Palestinian-controlled side of the Israeli checkpoint near Bethlehem. The morning was hot like every other, but the sun reflecting off the concrete checkpoint building and towering Separation Wall turned the immediate area into a reverberatory furnace. Tamer was waiting next to a black Toyota amid a sea of yellow taxicabs. He employed a series of exuberant hand gestures to gain our attention. Having awaited our arrival for some time, his fashionably upright tufts of dark brown hair glistened with sweat. A navy and white striped polo shirt clung to his body. Despite his soggy appearance, Tamer was as cheerful as he'd been the previous week at the Siraj Center and greeted us with spongy hugs. As Mark and I wriggled into the back seat of the broiling two-door compact, Tamer introduced us to the driver, a young Palestinian friend of his named Nabil.

From the checkpoint, we drove south through Bethlehem on a street divided by a narrow esplanade, freshly landscaped with rows of trees and flowering shrubs. On either side of the road was an eclectic mix of structures, some modern, others remnants of the past. Contemporary white stone buildings with bustling ground-floor shops, second-floor apartments with picture windows, and third-floor terraces sporting satellite dishes stood alongside crumbling masonry and concrete with peeling paint, rusted metal awnings, and soot-covered facades plastered with weathered posters of Yasser Arafat.

As Nabil navigated the Monday morning traffic, Tamer turned and faced Mark and me. "Look at this here," he said, his voice rising several decibels as he pointed to the steady progression of cars on the road and the people walking along the sidewalks. Honking horns and blaring music from car radios, an exotic fusion of classic Arabic and hip-hop, threatened to drown out his commentary. "The people are living their life. And they are determined about one thing. No matter what Israel is planning to do, we will still live our lives. We insist on living our lives. I can say that because everybody knows what Israel wants. They want us to leave the land. Every time they do something, the main goal is to force the Palestinians to leave the land. So it's not going to happen."

On the southern edge of Bethlehem, we pulled into the gravel parking lot of the Dheisheh Refugee Camp, stopping in front of the camp's Ibdaa Cultural Center. Beyond the narrow, multistory stone building housing the Ibdaa, I could see an agglomeration of concrete and cinderblock apartments, one stacked atop another—some three or four stories, others a precarious five or six. Steel bars encased a multitude of small, square windows set at irregular intervals. Exterior staircases zigzagged to upper floors. Red and black cables snaked in and out of exterior walls from one apartment to another. Rusted rebar shot up from flat rooftops, where gray steel water tanks served as clothesline anchors and bed linens fluttered in the breeze.

Standing outside the Ibdaa, Tamer introduced us to the camp's program director. Shadi, who was probably in his mid-thirties, wore a blue button-down shirt and a pair of pressed jeans, and he had neatly trimmed black hair and a close-shaven beard. He did not fit any image of a refugee I might have previously conjured.

Shadi explained that Dheisheh was one of dozens of camps set up by the United Nations to provide for Palestinians who had lost their homes to Israel as a result of the Arab-Israeli conflict of 1948. Of the 750,000 Palestinians who were forced or fled from their villages in areas captured by the Israelis, about 3,400 settled in Dheisheh. When the refugees first arrived, they lived in tents, thinking they were experiencing a temporary disruption and that they would soon return to their villages inside Israel. The United Nations had, after all, adopted a resolution stating that the refugees should be permitted to return to their homes at the earliest practicable date. But Israeli forces barred reentry of the refugees, destroyed hundreds of Palestinian villages, and repopulated remaining Palestinian villages with immigrants from Eastern Europe. It had been more than sixty years since the mass expulsion and exodus of Palestinians from their homeland, which Palestinians call the *Nabka* (Arabic for "catastrophe"). With population growth since the Nabka, there were now more than five million Palestinian refugees, about a third living in refugee camps in the Palestinian territories, Jordan, Lebanon, and Syria.

"Over time the refugees' tents were replaced with more permanent dwellings," Shadi said as he pointed to the jumble of concrete and cinderblock buildings around the Ibdaa, home to thirteen thousand people. "Traditionally, Palestinian families live together, and a son and wife build a house near the family house. But we can't do that here because the camp sits on just one square kilometer of land, and every inch is covered with structures, so we started to build on top—parents on the first floor, married kids on the second, and so on. Every time a floor is added, we leave rebar on top so it will be easy to add another apartment. Today there are five or six generations in one building, five or six floors." Shadi explained that the residents own the buildings, but not the land. "The land is leased by the United Nations from a Palestinian Jew." Shadi raised a hand in greeting to an elderly man who was watching us from an open window across the alley. "We have no problem with Jews, just with the Zionist movement."

A series of murals, some brightly painted in a primitive style, others skillfully drawn and haunting, spanned the inside of the cinderblock wall defining the camp's perimeter. "They are not just decorations," Shadi said. "The children of Dheisheh painted these. They depict what life was like in the forty-five villages the refugees left behind." He explained that they were expressions of the refugees' frustrations, their longing for home, sometimes marking hope for the future. Along with the children's murals were some painted by artists who had visited the camp. One of the largest and most arresting depicted a bulldozer made from a human skeleton that was stationed next to Israel's Separation Wall—it was one of many murals painted by the famous British graffiti artist Banksy, who called Palestine "the world's largest open-air prison and the ultimate activity holiday destination for graffiti artists."

Shadi led us through the camp's damp and narrow alleys, which coiled around the gray buildings. The flash of a camera startled me. I was so focused on the improbable cinderblock towers and the bleak images in the murals that I'd nearly forgotten Mark. Children, very curious about his camera, gathered around him, calling out, "Hallo, hallo," and trying to get his attention. Mark handed the camera to one of the young boys, who took a picture of his little brother sandwiched between us on the doorstep to their home. Other children zigzagged around us on bicycles. "There is no open space here for them to play, no parks, no playgrounds," Shadi said. "Inside the refugee camp there's nothing green, nothing but concrete." Watching the children, who seemed to multiply in number every few seconds, I had no doubt that they found outlets for their joys and mischief at every opportunity, even among these austere canyons of concrete. Had he grown up here, Mark would have been scaling the walls of the six-story buildings, visiting with families through their open windows on his way up.

Continuing our walk, Shadi showed us one of several portraits painted on apartment facades of residents killed by Israeli soldiers. It depicted a seventeen-year-old boy who had gone outside the camp to purchase a bag of concrete mix. The errand for his father was the last thing he would ever attempt; he was mistakenly shot by Israeli soldiers. Shadi said many innocent Dheisheh residents had died at the hands of Israeli soldiers. One young man was shot and killed while repairing his car after curfew. In Dheisheh, all those who died as a result of the conflict with Israel were elevated to martyr status, including three from the camp who died in suicide attacks on Israel. The idea of suicide bombing was abhorrent to me. Visceral images I'd seen in news accounts, amplified in my imagination by my concern for Mark, had propelled me on this trip and, at the same time, nearly kept me from boarding the plane. After our time in Hebron and now touring Dheisheh, I was beginning to understand how some might feel it was a last option, but I could never condone such violence. Rounding the corner, Shadi pointed to a blackened concrete structure piled high with rubble that spilled out into the alleyway from a jagged hole that was once a doorway. On the facade was a stencil of a young man and something written in Arabic. "When somebody from the family dies for Palestine, the family feels proud about it," Shadi explained. "The Israelis want to deny them their pride, so they destroy the homes of martyrs." As we walked on, I felt a deep sense of mourning for both sides, Palestinians and Israelis. So much of this suffering seemed completely needless and avoidable. (According to the Israeli human rights organization B'Tselem, between December 1987 and January 2009, 1,493 Israeli were killed by Palestinians, and 7,863 Palestinians were killed by Israelis.)

Just steps away, another structure had suffered a similar fate with its roof completely bombed off. It had been the home of a boy who was apprehended by the Israeli Defense Forces and shot in the head while in custody. "Because of his death, his three brothers joined the militant movement al-Aqsa Martyrs Brigades, and all three were arrested by the IDF. One is now serving twenty-seven life terms in Israeli prison, and the others, twenty-four life terms—that means twenty-seven times ninety-nine and twenty-four times ninety-nine, more than two thousand years each." Shadi described Israel's policy regarding jail terms, known as "the cemetery of numbers." "If a prisoner dies while serving a sentence, Israel buries the body in an Israeli cemetery and keeps it there until the full term has been served. Only then will the body be returned to the family." He said the bodies were often used by Israel for exchange. "For example, if Hezbollah kidnaps an Israeli soldier, Israel will negotiate with dead bodies for the release of the Israeli soldier." Looking back at the bombed-out house, Shadi said the rubble remained as a memorial to the martyrs; such houses would never be rebuilt.

We followed Shadi back through the concrete towers to the Cultural Center near the camp's entrance. He explained that the name "Ibdaa" translated from Arabic as "to create something out

of nothing." The Ibdaa opened in 1994, the first community center created inside a refugee camp anywhere in the Middle East.
Before 1994, Dheisheh and other refugee camps in the Palestinian
territories were prohibited by Israeli military order from operating
community centers or formal gathering sites or from building any
structure higher than one story. The Israeli military also barred
vehicles from entering the camp and banned books and newspapers inside homes. "We are thankful things are different today,"
Shadi said. He explained that after the bans were lifted, Dheisheh
residents formed committees to improve conditions at the camp.
These committees paved alleys and constructed water and sewer
lines—and built a daycare center, medical clinic, library, computer
training center, and two schools. Residents now even had Internet access. The committees also provided organized activities for
residents. "Our basketball teams, both men's and women's, have
won Palestinian championships, and one of our swimmers came
in second in the Arab world." Shadi made no attempt to stifle his
pride. "Many of our activities are connected to the refugees' right
to return to their ancestral villages. Through music and dance, the
children can express what it is like to live as a refugee and how
their families lived before losing their homes." Then Shadi turned
to Mark. "Dheisheh has one of the most famous music groups
in Palestine and two hip-hop groups, 'Badluck' and 'The Refugee
Rappers'—your readers would like these groups." I realized that
we might already have experienced a taste of the Dheisheh hip-
hop movement during our drive to the camp.

Shadi explained that one of the goals of the Ibdaa was to
educate Israel, Palestine, and the world about the plight of the

refugees. Families displaced during the 1948 Arab-Israeli conflict, and the generations who followed, would remain at the camp until they could return to their ancestral villages. "Even many Palestinians are not familiar with refugee camps. The president of the Palestinian Authority, Mahmoud Abbas, has made only one visit to a refugee camp."

I was surprised to learn that Dheisheh received no financial support, goods, or services from the Palestinian Authority. Many countries offered aid, but the camp refused assistance except from countries that remained neutral in the Israeli-Palestinian conflict. Japan, for instance, donated funds for Dheisheh's medical center. "Wherever you go in the world, most of the conflicts, in one way or another, are connected to what's going on here—the Palestinian-Israeli conflict has become like a hanger, and everyone in the world takes sides and says, 'I do it for Palestinians' or 'I do it for Israelis' and we don't want to be a hanger any more," Shadi said. "This is why we refuse help from both sides, and only accept it from those in the middle."

While we were congregated outside the Ibdaa, a volunteer from Italy joined our group. Filippo, a project manager for Italy's Association for the Cooperation among People, had a slight build, short curly brown hair, a small mustache, and big eyes. He was a far better dressed individual than I expected to find in a refugee camp—like Shadi, but with that inimitable Italian flair. "Of all of them," Mark told me later, "I was the one who looked most like a refugee." Shadi said Dheisheh received many international volunteers, and most were, like Filippo, from Italy. Shadi, who was born and raised in the refugee camp, told us he'd recently moved to an apartment in Beit Sahour. "Of the twenty flats in my building, sixteen are rented by Italians," he said laughing. "When we're finished with the Israeli occupation, for sure we'll have an Italian occupation."

The Ibdaa, we discovered, had several bunk rooms and a restaurant for visitors to the camp. Guest rooms in a refugee camp? Mark quickly poised his pen over a purple notebook. "What's the price of a room for one night?"

Does a refugee camp add value to a student travel guide of Israel and the Palestinian territories? I did not think it was possible at first. But as we departed Dheisheh, it occurred to me that one cannot possibly understand the Palestinian perspective, or even the region's travel inconveniences, without visiting this epicenter of the Palestinian experience. It certainly had touched Mark, and I had no doubt he would be staying in one of those rooms at the Ibdaa before the end of his work in the Palestinian territories. At fifty shekels (about twelve dollars) a night, the accommodations at this refugee camp were, as Mark put it, "an affordable luxury."

Thou Shalt Not Steal

Monday, July 6, afternoon.

Though the restaurant in the Dheisheh Refugee Camp would have been perfectly acceptable, Mark wanted to see several additional places that had been recommended by local people he'd met. As for me, I was feeling a new sense of urgency in these last hours of my trip and wanted to experience as much as I could before my flight home the following day. My travels with Mark over the past two weeks had opened up my awareness of the Palestinian people and their history and culture. The West Bank, a region that not long ago I'd considered fraught with danger and unworthy of travel, had become a most compelling place. I wanted to see more.

Our first stop was Qa'abar's, a restaurant in the older part Beit Jala, a predominantly Christian Palestinian village north of Bethlehem. The place was filled nearly to capacity when we arrived, and Tamer, Nabil, Mark, and I squeezed around the one small table that was open. We almost had to shout to hear one another over the room full of high-spirited conversations in Arabic. While I once might have felt anxious lingering in a West Bank café surrounded by loud Arabic voices, I now took the sounds to be congenial and to mean, "Hey, pass me another napkin," or "You should see this year's grape harvest!" Mark ordered the Palestinian-style barbecue for which Qa'abar's is famous, a moist, charcoal-grilled chicken pungent with cinnamon and clove. The aroma was almost enough to temporarily tempt me away from my vegetarian convictions. Mark found it wholly unforgettable.

Back in the car, we drove to another restaurant that Mark hoped to review for *Let's Go*. I think, honestly, if it had been left entirely up to Mark, he would have reviewed every single restaurant in Israel and the West Bank. Perhaps there was a bit of chef inside my budding computer scientist. Certainly there was a healthy appetite. Barbra Restaurant was set on a hilltop in the outskirts of Beit Jala. The three brothers who owned Barbra (and lived in the family home on the floor below the restaurant) had recently renovated the dining and bar areas. Although it wasn't open for business when we stopped by (Mark would return later to review the food), one of the brothers gave us a tour and showed us the handcrafted wood and tile work, which gave the interior a cozy yet cosmopolitan feel. The restaurant's windows provided a cinematic vantage point from which patrons could gaze across the surrounding hills, and Tamer called us over to take in the view of Israeli settlements encroaching on Beit Jala's terraced hillsides and agricultural land. Pointing to bulldozers leveling hills that once grew grapes and olives, he told us that Israel had already taken over two-thirds of the village's land to build Israeli settlements and to expand the boundaries of Jerusalem. Although the entire area is located on the West Bank side of the Green Line, Israel planned to include it on the Israeli side of the Separation Wall—and in the process take hundreds of additional acres of Beit Jala's land. "The path of the Separation Wall cuts right through the village and will isolate one part of the village from the other. It will isolate farmers from their farmland. Farming is their livelihood. Without their farmland they have nothing."

From Barbra Restaurant, Tamer navigated as Nabil drove along a narrow, winding road to Beit Jala's Cremisan Monastery. The monastery had been built a century ago by the Roman Catholic Salesians of Don Bosco. A seminary for international theology students preparing for the order stood among the carefully tended gardens, cypress trees, grape trellises, and olive groves reminiscent of Tuscany. On the lighter side, the Salesians also operated a winery, Cremisan Cellars, where they produced wine and brandy from grapes purchased from local Palestinian farmers. Nabil pulled into a small lot, and Mark set off with his camera to photograph the monastery for his next *Let's Go* copy batch. Later, Mark and I reunited inside Cremisan Cellars for a wine tasting, departing with a bottle each of chardonnay and cabernet. As we were leaving, Tamer said that the Cremisan winery was the sole source of income for most of the Palestinian farmers who sold grapes in this region, and as was true for other Palestinian farmers, their livelihood was being now threatened by Israel's Separation Wall. "Israeli bulldozers came through the olive groves and uprooted ancient trees near Cremisan to make way for the Separation Wall. The path cuts right through the monastery grounds and puts the main building on the Israeli side of the wall." I turned back to watch the monastery grow distant, appearing as an oasis in our rear window as we drove on through the dry land and dusty constructions sites where the Israeli Separation Wall and Israeli settlements rose from the Palestinian farmlands.

Our next stop was the Tent of Nations, a center for peaceful activism on a hilltop farm southwest of Bethlehem. Though not on his official itinerary, Mark thought its significant volunteer opportunities and rustic accommodations would be a valuable addition to *Let's Go*. The night before, while we were up late talking, Mark had told me that he had enjoyed the times we encountered the crux of the Palestinian/Israeli conflict far more than the spas and light shows we'd seen—at least he found them more meaningful. Our trip to the Tent of Nations would be another one of those times.

The drive to the Tent of Nations took us southwest of Beit Jala and Bethlehem and through the Palestinian farming village Nahalin. While Nabil drove, Tamer told us the story of Tent of Nations. Nearly a century ago, when the region was ruled by the Turks, a Palestinian Christian named Daher Nassar purchased the hundred-acre farm. Daher, and his sons and grandsons after him, worked the land during the day, planting olive, grape, and apple trees, and slept in a cave dug out of the hilltop at night. After the Israeli occupation, Israel began taking Palestinian land in the area around the Nassar farm for Israeli settlements, and in 1991, the Israeli military attempted to appropriate the Nassar farm by declaring the farm "state land." (I later read, in a report published by the Israeli human rights organization B'Tselem, that this was a common practice: Israel had taken control of more than half the land in the West Bank, mainly for establishing and expanding Israeli settlements, and the mechanism most often employed was declaring land "state land"—a method B'Tselem concluded was a ploy to conceal Israel's continued theft of land in the West Bank.) The Nassar family challenged Israel's attempt to take their land in a case that dragged on for many years in the Israeli court system, from military to civil, and cost the Nassars a significant amount of money. It was a slow, costly, and painful process that I imagined rivaled that of the English Court of Chancery's handling of *Jarndyce and Jarndyce* in Charles Dickens's *Bleak House*. The Nassar family fought all the way up to the Supreme Court of Israel, where they presented the court with stacks of ancient land records dating back to the Ottoman Empire that provided irrefutable proof of their title to the land—a feat made possible by financial assistance from their church in Nahalin and by technical assistance from one of Israel's top surveyors, who traveled from London to Istanbul in search of the ancient records. In 2007, after sixteen years of litigation, Israel's state attorney decided to discontinue the case before the Supreme Court handed down a decision. In the midst of the legal battle, one of Daher Nassar's grandchildren, Daoud, founded the Tent of Nations. The Nassars set aside part of their farm for the center, which is run by Daoud and his brother Daher, along with other family members and many volunteers.

From Nahalin, Nabil turned the black Toyota onto a partially paved road that wound precipitously up the rocky hillside of the Nassar farm. Near the top, the four of us abandoned the car along with the dust cloud that had followed us up the road and walked a short path to the rocky plateau. We paused briefly at a circular limestone terrace bounded by stone pews, bracing ourselves against the winds threatening to topple us. The open-air sanctuary offered a panoramic view of the surrounding hilltops and the sprawling Israeli settlements ringing the farm. One hilltop settlement was situated so close I didn't need binoculars to take in the rows of terracotta roofed white stone mansions and the frames of yet more under construction. The Israeli settlements, most built on land belonging to Palestinian farming villages like Nahalin, were on the West Bank side of the Green Line, yet the Israeli Separation Wall would put them—along with the Nassar farm and Nahalin—on the Israeli side of the wall. Tamer watched as Israeli bulldozers clearing the land rumbled and cracked beneath spreading layers of a low-hanging haze composed of soil that once fed Palestinian families. "Welcome to Palestine," he said. "This is Palestine."

We were joined at the scenic overlook by Daher Nassar, grandson of the elder Daher. It was nearly impossible to guess his age. This life was hard and afforded few comforts. I tried to count generational ages backward through the hundred years his family had farmed this land. His hair and mustache were graying but his tanned, lined face broke into a wide and youthful smile when he saw us. He lifted his green baseball cap to me when introduced. Daher welcomed us warmly and explained more details of the project and the challenges they faced. "The Israelis want our farm to expand their settlement," he said, looking around at the nearby hilltop. "The settlers have threatened us with guns, attacked us, and dumped out our water tanks. Three times they've come with bulldozers to build their own roads through our land, and one night they uprooted two hundred fifty of our olive trees." Since then volunteers at the Tent of Nations had helped the Nassars plant more than five hundred trees, many of which were paid for by a group called European Jews for a Just Peace in Palestine. "We invited people to come here to plant trees because if the Israeli military sees no trees on land then they can take the land."

We followed Daher to the tent that served as the sleeping quarters for visitors to the Tent of Nations. Crossing the plateau, we made a colorful if odd parade: Mark with his green daypack slung over his shoulder and red paisley bandana tied around his head; Tamer in his tight navy and white polo and black slacks; me in a yellow synthetic shirt, stretchy black skirt, and blue plastic flip-flops; and Nabil tagging behind in a pink polo shirt and jeans. The wind swirled and eddied around us, dusting us with fine sand that blew into our eyes and mouths when we were not careful to shield them. I was startled by the sudden appearance of a stallion galloping just feet away from us, whinnying as it passed, much to Mark's delight. Far less startling, yet wholly unexpected, was a long, exultant crow from an unseen rooster. We should have learned by now to suspend all expectations.

Viewed from afar, the long green tent gave the dry, rocky land the aura of a desert oasis. Inside, an American volunteer named Kat, who had curly blond hair and wore a "Milburn 2008" tee shirt, was preparing for the arrival of a church group from the United States. Daher made introductions, and Mark immediately struck up a conversation and casual interview with Kat about her job, how she came here, and her impressions of the Nassars' project. He took notes for *Let's Go* while she changed bed linens on narrow cots arranged in two rows along the lengths of the tent. Strong afternoon sunlight pierced the tarp and cast a lime hue on the assorted paisleys and plaids, as well as on all of us, while the winds rapped the sides of the tarp. The entire structure rattled.

As we set out to tour the farm, Daher said the family had wanted to construct a guesthouse to replace the tent, but they were unable to obtain a building permit. The farm lay in Area C—that 60 percent of the West Bank under Israeli military control and civil administration—where Palestinians are prohibited from building without an Israeli permit. Unable to secure construction permits to build above ground, the Nassars refurbished the original cave and built two additional caves, which served as meeting rooms, classrooms, and worship areas. Daher led us to the old cave, where he had once lived with his mother and father. Stone stairs descended into the dark, cool room. A single bulb suspended from the ceiling illuminated paintings on the cave's walls—portraits of Daher's father and grandfather and a mural that Daher said depicted "Christian, Muslim, and Jewish coming together to talk about peace." In another cave, a stone staircase opened into a spacious room with wooden benches along the perimeter, a stone floor cut from boulders on the farm and laid by hand in a circular pattern, and a ceiling painted sky blue around a yellow star of Bethlehem, an emblem of their Christian faith. Afterward, we followed Daher to the underground grotto, where they stabled horses, chickens, and pigeons. All of these living, working, and devotional spaces carved into the rock beneath the earth gave the impression that the Nassars lived under siege. And, in a sense, they did.

The Nassar farm was not connected to the power grid or public water supply. Because Israel refused to grant the Nassars permits for building any permanent infrastructure, the family had installed a small, gasoline-powered generator to provide a few hours of electricity each day. They purchased drinking water, which was trucked in from Nahalin and stored in cisterns on the farm. Daher strode across the dusty ground to show us several other projects. One was a rainwater collection system being built by a young German volunteer. Shirtless, tanned, and muscular with shoulder-length blond hair, he stood waist-deep in the hole, cementing the sides as we talked to him. I imagined that he was a pleasant distraction for the female volunteers on site. A second project, nearly finished, was a rustic yet practical bathroom: toilets made of wood planks with holes set above a collection area, where the human waste was gathered and formed into bricks for use as compost. These were projects I could see Mark completing, as I imagined his wilderness survival courses had exposed him to some fairly primitive "amenities."

After our tour of the Tent of Nations, Daher invited us to stay for tea. We all took seats at a long wooden picnic table, shielded on one side from the persistent wind by a wall with a mosaic-tiled biblical scene of three camels guided by the Star of Bethlehem. A volunteer from Russia, about my age, served us warm black tea in small glasses garnished with sage leaves grown on the farm. She sat with us and sipped a glass of tea, as did Kat and the shirtless young German, whose skin was still lightly flecked with bits of dried cement. As dusk settled atop the plateau in the fertile farmlands southwest of Bethlehem, Daher talked about peace. "We want to have peace, Christian, Muslim, and Jewish altogether," he said. "We resist evil with good; we refuse to be enemies."

The sun was low, painting streaks of violet and orange on the horizon as we made our way back to the Israeli checkpoint near

Bethlehem. As Nabil drove, Mark and Tamer talked, and I looked out the window, taking in this part of the world for the very last time. I watched as lights began to switch on in the hilltop mansions of Israeli settlers. Looking back at the Nassar farm, an unlit, black hill against a graying sky, I felt tranquility in the darkness.

The Sherut at Jaffa Gate

Tuesday, July 7.

On my last day in the Middle East, I woke to complete silence, something rare in the heart of Jerusalem's Old City. In our room at the Lutheran Guesthouse, Mark slept in his bed, motionless. I propped my head up on a pillow, contemplating my afternoon departure. Yousef had insisted on arranging a ride for me via *sherut*, the customary Israeli shared taxi-van, which I was to meet outside the Jaffa Gate. The sherut would take me to the Tel Aviv airport, where I'd catch a flight to Newark. From there, I would board my connecting flight to Austin. I pictured Rex and Paul at the Austin airport, waiting for me at the foot of the escalator near baggage claim. They were a matched set, both well over six feet tall, lanky, with sandy hair falling in their eyes. At every still moment in my trip, I had missed them. Now, as I prepared to leave this place, I missed them even more. I couldn't wait to hear every detail of their past two weeks of adventure—from the Coast Mountains of Alaska to the WinStar Casino of the Chickasaw Nation.

Still in bed, I turned my thoughts back to Mark, sleeping just across the room. Once again, we had talked nearly through the night about our experiences over the past week in the West Bank, this time while sitting at a table on the patio of the Lutheran Guesthouse, drinking the wine we'd purchased at Cremisan Cellars. We talked about the Dheisheh Refugee Camp and the children's murals of their ancestral villages, most, if not all, long destroyed or repopulated with Jewish immigrants. Would the children live forever as refugees? What about their children? We talked about the Tent of Nations and the Nassar family's continuing struggle to keep Israel from appropriating their land. How long could the Nassars hold out? How long would the aging canvas tent hold out? We talked about the Palestinian villages Beit Jala and Nahalin and about the farmland taken for Israeli settlements. How would the Palestinian farmers make a living in the years to come? We discussed the path of Israel's Separation Wall and how it doesn't even follow the Green Line, the internationally recognized boundary of Israel, but instead meanders wildly through Palestinian lands, dividing Palestinian villages and isolating Palestinian farmers from their farmland. We talked about the Palestinian farmers of Khirbet Safa. Would their farm forever remain an Israeli "closed military zone"? Would it someday become an Israeli settlement? And what about the Al-Azzehs, the Palestinian family we met in Tel Rumeida? How long would they be able to tolerate life in Hebron's inner city, surrounded by one hundred Israeli roadblocks, rooftop monitoring towers, and checkpoints on the ground, not to mention gun-toting Jewish settlers and both stink water and nasty graffiti? What about the "man-made" drought Israel had caused in the West Bank? The identification cards Israel required Palestinians to carry? The Israeli roadblocks and checkpoints—and flying checkpoints—on Palestinian roads? The building permits that

Palestinians routinely applied for and Israel routinely refused to grant? By the time we got back to the room and I climbed into bed, I felt disheartened and exhausted. Yes, there was nothing better than the enormous baobab at Ein Gedi Kibbutz to represent the complexities of the region. The issues were too large for one person to embrace, and as an outsider, I could not possibly understand all the history, desires, fears, and aspirations of the Israeli people or the Palestinian people. But for me, no matter where one stood on the broader issues, one thing was certain: George was right. Israel's policies and actions in the West Bank were gradually wearing down the Palestinian people, making their life so miserable that they want to leave. This was especially true in the 60 percent of the West Bank that is in Area C and under "temporary" Israeli military and civil control, where Israel's policies and actions focused on establishing a permanent Israeli or Jewish presence, while expediting the exodus of Palestinians.

After Mark woke up, we had breakfast together at the guesthouse, followed by a leisurely walk through the Old City. When we returned to the guesthouse, I packed for my departure. I folded all I had brought with me back into my small black suitcase. I carefully wrapped the one keepsake I'd purchased, Nisreen Al-Azzeh's pastel of the severed olive trees, and cushioned it between two folded knit tops. I would wear the blue flip-flops on the plane. I also packed a few things that Mark wanted me to take back to Austin: two black and white keffiyehs similar to the one worn by Yasser Arafat, gifts for Rex and Paul, and the Gatorade bottle filled with Dead Sea mud, a gift for Beryl. Mark's thinking, no doubt, was that I would be more successful than he passing through the tight security at the Tel Aviv airport carrying that bottle of black ooze.

After packing, I hugged Mark goodbye. While I had almost come to take his presence for granted, I could already feel the tug of missing him creeping up on me. I told him and he was touched. But Mark was so full of energy focused on his assignment—his official and unofficial activities—that I doubted he would miss me nearly as much. George had invited Mark to spend a few days at his family's home in Beit Sahour and join the festivities marking the end of the first term of the Palestinian Summer Celebration. After that, Mark planned to move into a bunk room at the Dheisheh Refugee Camp. When his work in the Bethlehem area was completed, Mark's job for *Let's Go* would take him to other Palestinian-controlled cities, including Ramallah, Nablus, and Jericho. My incessant checking for news reports during our trip rendered those names unforgettable. But I was no longer worried about Mark's safety. The words "Palestinian," "terrorist," and "suicide bomber" were no longer intertwined in my mind. I was confident Mark would make his way safely and enthusiastically around the West Bank. He would follow Rex's advice. He would not let opportunities pass untaken. He would accept challenges and throw himself into activities requiring energy and focus. And, after he submitted his last copy batch for *Let's Go*, I was confident he would make it safely on that plane to Paris, where he'd spend his days and evenings with Beryl at cheap cafés, Asian grocery stores, inexpensive wineries, and cinemas that played only French new wave.

As the sherut taking me on my final Israeli road trip (for the foreseeable future) departed from the gate, Mark boarded a

Palestinian bus to the Israeli checkpoint near Bethlehem. I was no longer worried about Mark's safety, yet I was wistful, perhaps a little sad. My son was all grown up. I was no longer essential to his well-being. I knew somewhere in my heart that the same was also true of Paul, who shortly after my return to Austin would be leaving home for college. Rex and I had spent more than twenty years working for our children's passage to independence. The time, which should be cause for celebration, was here. I pressed my palm against the window of the sherut, watching the ecru minarets and muted silver domes of Jerusalem's Old City grow small and indistinguishable, missing my boys terribly.

Postscript:
Coyotes Howling at the
Bloodmobile Door

September 10, 2010.

It has been over a year since my trip to Israel and the Palestinian territories. The day I returned home, Rex, sporting a new beard, and Paul, his hair trail-shaggy, met me at the airport and launched into an animated account of their three weeks together. That evening, we watched videos of all thirty-three miles of their hike from the Coast Mountains of Alaska to the Yukon Territory of British Columbia, while Rex narrated *National Geographic*-style. There were tense sequences of Paul, in his Peruvian hat, trekking over the snow-covered Chilkoot pass, careful to keep some distance from the others in the event of an avalanche, and again of Paul, this time crossing a primitive suspension bridge that wobbled high above a rocky gorge. He had won a bet by traversing it without using his hands. There was even footage of their guide, Roger, whose backpack spanned from above his head to the back of his knees, and who walked with a spring in his step a good twenty feet ahead of Rex and Paul even when there was no avalanche threat. From time to time, Roger looked back to offer encouragement and advice like "snow can be your friend" and "try not to fall down to the rocks," and every time he saw the camera pointed at him, he who would sing out loudly, "Hello Austin!"

Once Rex and Paul finally exhausted their supply of stories, they were eager to hear the details of my travels. I recounted my harrowing drive across the narrow stretch of desert between the West Bank and Gaza, and my unlikely reunion with Mark in Arad. I told them about Mark bobbing like a cork in the Dead Sea and then slathering his body with mud, and about the worrisome sinkholes. I told them about the lush gardens of Ein Gedi Kibbutz, the nighttime botanical garden tour, and Zabu's comparing President Obama to the enormous baobab tree. These stories were easy to tell. They were short vignettes of memorable moments that required little other explanation. But when I turned to my travels with Mark in the West Bank, my accounts became long, convoluted, and considerably less entertaining. How could I tell Rex and Paul about my drive with Mark to the Israeli beaches in the Jordan Valley of the Palestinian West Bank without telling them that Israel routinely bars Palestinians from entering those beaches and that Israel had absorbed and "de facto" annexed those beaches and most of the other land in the West Bank's Jordan Valley—land that was designated more than sixty years ago for a new Arab state and is still recognized by every other country in the world as part of a future Palestinian state? How could I tell them about my lunch with Mark, Jana, and Hisham at the Freedom Coffee Shop in the Palestinian city of Hebron without explaining that the coffee shop's very existence is an act of peaceful resistance against the Israeli occupation, which had, with its thousands of Israeli soldiers and hundreds of checkpoints, road closures, and video surveillance cameras, run out more than 80 percent of the Palestinian residents and businesses and caused the economic collapse of Hebron's entire city center? I felt the same way about the Dheisheh Refugee Camp, the Tent of Nations, and every other place we had visited in the West Bank. I needed to explain the significance of those places, and even my iPhone videos required a lot of explaining. A genuine understanding of those places demanded, at the very least, some knowledge of the region's geopolitical subtleties.

My challenge was to figure out how to convey an image of those places and their importance so I could share my experiences with Rex and Paul and my mother, sisters, and friends. I wanted to open a window through which, going forward, they could listen for the other side of the story, the one seldom heard in our Western media. I found that I could not rest until I had done so. The most direct way for me to do this was by writing about my journey, from beginning to end.

Writing this story has occupied much of the past year. My travel journal and videos have helped immensely, enabling me to describe my trip as accurately as possible. When I first sat down to write, I did not realize that it would take so much time to recount the story of my journey, and I had no expectation that it would one day be published.

Though I made the trip out of an instinctive need to assure myself of my son's safety, I suspect I was also motivated by an unacknowledged desire for adventure in a life that was smooth and predictable, as well as a curiosity about a land close to my birthplace. It was the first time Mark and I had traveled together as adults, and I thoroughly enjoyed every blister, every dusty bus ride, every new opportunity to become reacquainted with him. My adventures with Mark took me far beyond my earlier research and understanding of the Israeli and Palestinian people and the Israeli occupation of the Palestinian territories. The complexities of the region are overwhelming and difficult to embrace, like the trunk of the enormous baobab at Ein Gedi that Zabu calls the Obama tree and that I, over the past year, have come to call the "wisdom tree." In the story of my journey, I could not, and do not attempt to, write about all the issues and divergent points of view in the region. *Let's Go* set Mark's itinerary, and I tagged along with him for the two weeks I was there. My story is about the places we visited, the people we met, and what I learned along the way. What I witnessed left me in agreement with most Palestinians—and many Israelis—who believe that Israel's appropriation of Palestinian land and discriminatory treatment of the Palestinian people are illegal and unjust.

In September 2009, after his summer assignment for *Let's Go* and his Paris vacation with Beryl, Mark returned to Harvard for the 2009–2010 school year. Paul, his gap year finally over, joined Mark in Cambridge to begin his freshman year at Harvard.

At the conclusion of the 2009–2010 school year, Mark was still one semester short of graduation because he had taken time off to work for a professor. The Harvard Dean's Office, however, let him walk at the May 2010 commencement ceremony, his diploma to follow once he completed his final semester. My

mother and sisters joined Rex, Paul, Mark, and me at the ceremony, collectively bestowing on Mark gift checks totaling $1,350.
Days later, Mark signed the checks over to Murphy's Used Cars
for the title to an old red and white Chevy Astro van. On close
inspection, one can still see the stenciled name of the former
owner, the New York Blood Bank. Mark shoved a mattress and
some of his belongings into the back of the "bloodmobile," as he
calls it, and drove to Cape Cod for his summer job at the Woods
Hole Oceanographic Institution (WHOI). Housing on the Cape
is expensive, and Mark decided to save money by sleeping in the
bloodmobile, which he kept in a small wooded parking area next
to his lab at WHOI. His supervisor, apparently comfortable with
the arrangement, gave him a key to the building, where there was a
bathroom and kitchen that Mark could use in the evenings.

Harvard's 2010–2011 school year began last week, and Paul,
having spent his summer researching lizards in Panama, is back in
Cambridge, embarking on his sophomore year. But Mark is still in
Cape Cod; he enjoyed his summer job so much that he decided to
take a leave of absence from school to continue at WHOI, with a
promise to complete his final semester in the spring.

Tonight, after sending my editor the first complete draft of
my book, I called Mark to give him the good news. He answered
his cell phone from the back of the bloodmobile, where he was
reading a book about Kant by the light of a citronella candle. The
weather on Cape Cod is getting colder, and I asked whether he
was warm enough sleeping in the van. Yes, he said, he had blankets
so I shouldn't worry. He said the job at WHOI was going well,
and there was something about a computer program he had been

working on for an underwater robot, but I could barely hear him over the wailing chorus of high-pitched voices in the background. "It's just the coyotes," Mark told me. "There's a pack of coyotes on either side of the parking lot, and they howl all night long."

I'm picturing my son alone in the bloodmobile with the cold winds blowing across the Cape and hungry coyotes howling in the woods around him. And my only thought is, *He will be fine.*

Acknowledgements

Many people helped with this book, though none are responsible for the views in it. I am so very grateful to my editors, Nancy Ford, who worked with me on the first drafts of the manuscript, and Mia Ortman, who worked with me on the final drafts. They both made this book possible. Their encouragement and guidance kept me writing to completion, and their insight and wit helped bring to life the journal I kept during my travels. I am grateful also for the comments of the many people who were kind enough to take their time to read various drafts of my manuscript and share their thoughts, including Jim George, Ken Gormley, Spencer Johnson, Rayda Porter, Rose Ann Reeser, Sabra Sweeney, and Mary Tucker—and also Erika Fine, who provided me with another perspective on many issues in the course of her very quick and skillful final edit. I am grateful as well to those mentioned in this book who unwittingly helped by becoming part of my story, several for whom I use pseudonyms.

I am forever thankful to my wonderful family: my husband, Rex VanMiddlesworth, our sons, Mark and Paul, my mother, Patricia Gray, and my sisters, Sheri, Cathy, and Sandy, and their families. Thank you Rex for the updates from Alaska and the Chickasaw Nation and the advice you gave our sons upon their departure for college, much of which made its way into this book, and for reading many manuscript drafts and providing helpful suggestions. Thank you especially for picking up dinner to-go on your way home from work those countless evenings I spent writing. Thank you Mark for taking that job you were so excited about with *Let's Go*—and for calling home to let us know that you had been kidnapped by Bedouins. Thank you also for letting me travel with you, for being a delightful companion and intrepid guide, and for all your help reviewing and commenting on manuscript drafts. Thank you Paul for agreeing to spend part of your gap year helping me. You were the most enjoyable companion and dutiful assistant, painstakingly making all those copies of the *Sunday Ghibli*—and then entertaining Dad and me with the stories about Libyan locust wars and such—who would have thought they'd end up in a book about Israel and the Palestinian territories? Thank you to my mother, the most positive of thinkers, who, long before the first draft was complete, visualized this book would be published, always asking "when" and never "if." Thank you to my sisters and everyone else for putting up with me when my book took precedence and for listening to my stories so many times that you probably can all recite them from memory.

This book is dedicated to my family for all of their love and support, and to the memory of my sister Linda and my father, Lt. General Stanley M. Umstead, Jr., who took us to the ends of the world and back.

Notes and Sources

Photographs from my travels with Mark in Israel and the Palestinian territories, along with news updates about the places we visited and the people we met, are on Facebook, https://www.facebook.com/TheWisdomTreeBook.

Bedouin Kidnappers

Mark was hired to write for the new edition of *Let's Go Israel and the Palestinian Territories*, one of more than forty *Let's Go's* guidebooks. The group that publishes *Let's Go* is part of Harvard Student Agencies, a corporation formed by Harvard in the 1950s to provide meaningful paying jobs for its students, and the guidebooks are entirely student-written. As *Let's Go* puts it, "With pen and notebook in hand and a few changes of underwear stuffed in our backpacks, we spend months roaming the globe in search of travel bargains," http://www.letsgo.com/.

The news about Israeli soldiers killing Islamic extremists caught planting an explosive near the Gaza border fence and the bomb exploding near an Israeli patrol vehicle was reported in "Israel: 2 Palestinian Militants Are Killed," *New York Times*, May

23, 2009, http://www.nytimes.com/2009/05/23/world/middleeast/23briefs-brfISRAEL.html?_r=0.

The clashes between Hamas and Fatah in the West Bank were reported in "Israeli Troops Kill Hamas Leader in West Bank," *Haaretz*, May 31, 2009, http://www.haaretz.com/print-edition/news/israeli-troops-kill-hamas-leader-in-west-bank-1.276963.

The news about Israeli soldiers killing a Palestinian man participating in a demonstration against Israel's Separation Wall was reported in "West Bank: Palestinian Killed in Demonstration," *New York Times*, June 6, 2009, http://www.nytimes.com/2009/06/06/world/middleeast/06briefs-Wbank.html.

The news about Israeli forces near Gaza killing four Palestinian gunmen spotted planting explosive devices along the Israel-Gaza border was reported in "Israel Kills 4 Gunmen on Gaza Line," *New York Times*, June 9, 2009, http://query.nytimes.com/gst/fullpage.html?res=9A05E4D91E3EF93AA35755C0A96F9C8B63.

Consider This Area Off-Limits When Planning Your Itinerary

The news about Palestinian militants from Gaza firing a Qassam rocket into Israel's Ashkelon Beach area and Israel attacking two tunnels under the Gaza-Egypt border was reported in "Israel Targets Smuggling Tunnels in Gaza," *CNN*, June 14, 2009, http://articles.cnn.com/2009-06-14/world/israel.tunnels_1_communities-in-southern-israel-rocket-and-mortar-attacks-gaza-egypt-border?_s=PM:WORLD.

The firing of the second Qassam rocket by Palestinian militants from Gaza was reported in "Second Kassam in 24 Hours Hits South," *Jerusalem Post,* June 16, 2009.

The UN General Assembly resolution partitioning Palestine, Resolution 181, was adopted on November 29, 1947. The resolution stated, in part: "The Independent Arab and Jewish States and the Special International Regime for the City of Jerusalem . . . shall come into existence in Palestine not later than 1 October 1948." The "Special International Regime for the City of Jerusalem" encompassed immediate surrounding areas, including Bethlehem. A copy of Resolution 181 is available on the website of the United Nations Information System on the Question of Palestine (UNISPAL), http://unispal.un.org/unispal.nsf/0/7F 0AF2BD897689B785256C330061D253.

The population and land statistics for Palestine are from Sandy Tolan's *The Lemon Tree: An Arab, a Jew, and the Heart of the Middle East* (New York: Bloomsbury, 2006), p. 49. *The Lemon Tree* is a nonfiction account of two families, one Arab and one Jewish, and covers the history of the conflict between Arabs and Jews in Palestine, the exodus of Arabs from Israeli-captured areas, and the immigration of Jews from Eastern Europe into the new Jewish state. According to the UN report from which the population statistics originated, the 1946 population of Palestine was 1,203,000 Arabs, 608,000 Jews, and 35,000 "other." The report, "UN Special Committee on Palestine Report to the General Assembly, Volume I," A/364, September 3, 1947, is available on the UNISPAL website, http://unispal.un.org/UNISPAL.NSF/ 0/07175DE9FA2DE563852568D3006E10F3.

The *Sunday Ghibli* was published in Tripolitania (a province that later became part of the UN-created country Libya) by the Government Press of the British Military Administration. I obtained microfilm copies of the weekly newspaper from the Center for Research Libraries, Chicago, Illinois. The articles I reference—and the issue number and date of the paper in which they appear—include the following: "Strife Continues in Palestine," No. 61, January 4, 1948; "Still More Palestine Outrages," "No Let Up in Reign of Lawlessness," No. 62, January 11, 1948; "Palestine Mandate Ends, 25 Years of British Achievement," "Jewish State Proclaimed," No. 80, May 16, 1948; "The Palestine Situation, UNO Cease Fire Order Refused," "America Criticizes Britain," No. 82, May 30, 1948; "UNO and Palestine, Mediator Tours Holy Land," No. 83, June 6, 1948; "Peace Returns to Palestine, UNO Truce Terms Accepted," No. 84, June 13, 1948; "The Palestine Panorama," No. 94, August 22, 1948; and, "United Nations Mediator Murdered in Palestine, Dastardly Crime Shocks the World," No. 98, September 19, 1948.

For information about the 1949 Armistice Agreements, I relied on Jimmy Carter's *We Can Have Peace in the Holy Land: A Plan That Will Work* (New York: Simon & Schuster, 2009), pp. 9-10.

During the 1967 Six-Day War, Israel also captured the Golan Heights from Syria, and the Golan Heights remains an Israeli-occupied territory. Unlike Gaza and the West Bank, the Golan Heights was not part of the land designated for the Arab state by UN Resolution 181 and thus is not considered part of the "Palestinian territories."

The UN Security Council resolution calling for Israel's withdrawal from the Palestinian territories, Resolution 242, was adopted on November 22, 1967, and is available on the UNISPAL website, http://unispal.un.org/unispal.nsf/0/7D35E1F72 9DF491C85256EE700686136.

The Oslo Accords include the following agreements: Declaration of Principles on Interim Self-Government Arrangements, September 13, 1993, a copy of which is available on the website of the UN Refugee Agency (UNHCR), http://www.unhcr.org/refworld/docid/3de5e96e4.html; Agreement on the Gaza Strip and the Jericho Area, April 29, 1994, which is available on the UNISPAL website, http://unispal.un.org/UNISPAL.NSF/0/15AF20B2F7F41905852560A7004AB2D5; and, The Interim Agreement on the West Bank and the Gaza Strip, September 28, 1995, which is available on the UNHCR website, http://www.unhcr.org/refworld/docid/3de5ebbc0.html.

I later read about Israel's expulsion of the Arabs from Lydda in Sandy Tolan's *The Lemon Tree*, p. 65. On July 12, 1948, Israeli Lieutenant Colonel Yitzhak Rabin issued the order, which stated in part: "The inhabitants of Lydda must be expelled quickly without attention to age." I read more about the expulsion in Benny Morris's *1948 and After* (New York: Oxford University Press, 2003) (same quote on p. 2).

The guidebooks quoted are *Fodor's Exploring Israel*, fourth edition (2007), p. 209, and *Lonely Planet, Israel & the Palestinian Territories*, fifth edition (2007), pp. 286, 289. I noted in my journal *Frommer's* advice to "consider this area off-limits" before discarding the guidebook because it was not helpful, though while preparing these notes, I found the quoted portion on the guidebook's website, http://www.frommers.com/destinations/israel/0227020814.html.

What is Hebrew for "Women's Restroom"?
In addition to information yielded from random Internet searches at the Newark airport, I read about Jewish religion and customs, the law of return, and immigration into Israel in *Lonely Planet, Israel & the Palestinian Territories*, fifth edition (2007), pp. 45, 47.

The Future Population of Arad is Fifty Thousand
After returning home, I researched what Mark said about immigration into Israel and confirmed that many immigrants do not consider themselves Jewish. For example, in 2009, about thirty thousand of the non-Arabs living in Be'er Sheva (which at the time was home to over sixty thousand Russian immigrants) did not identify themselves as Jewish. See, Israel Central Bureau of Statistics, "Statistical Abstract of Israel, 2010," No. 61, Subject 2, Table 16, http://www.cbs.gov.il/reader/shnaton/shnatone_new.htm?CYear=2010&Vol=61&CSubject=2.

Welcome to the Lowest Spot on Earth
The National Public Radio story about Fatah leaders claiming Hamas was plotting to take over the West Bank by force was "Palestinian Rift in the West Bank Intensifies" by Lourdes

Garcia-Navarro, which aired on June 23, 2009, http://www.npr.
org/templates/story/story.php?storyId=105782880.

A Bedouin Disneyland

Mark's description of the squalid Bedouin areas he saw while
on the bus en route to Be'er Sheva was confirmed by the report
"Invisible Citizens: Israeli Government Policy Toward the Negev
Bedouin," released by the Israeli nonpartisan policy analysis institute Adva Center in February 2006. According to the report,
seventy-six thousand Bedouin citizens of Israel lived in forty-five
settlements that had not been accorded governmental recognition
and did not appear on official maps of Israel. Some of those settlements were located in northeastern part of the Negev, between
Be'er Sheva, Arad, and Dimona, all places where Mark had been
working. The report said of these Bedouin settlements: "In about
half of the households there is no running water and residents
have to use a variety of methods to obtain water. The settlements
are not connected to electricity, so that there are no refrigerators
in most of the homes and there is no lighting in the streets. Like-
wise, the settlements lack a sewerage system, a fact that has severe
environmental and sanitary implications. Open rivers of sewerage
from neighboring Jewish towns traverse some of the settlements.
None of the localities has a waste disposal system." More information about the Adva Center is available on the organization's
website, as is a copy of the report, http://www.adva.org/default.
asp?pageid=5, http://www.adva.org/uploaded/NegevEnglish-
Summary.pdf.

Dead Sea Perils and Positive Energies

The story about Eli Raz being sucked into a sinkhole and the hiker was who was critically injured when he fell into a sinkhole near Ein Gedi was reported in "Dead Sea Sinkholes Swallow Up Plans: Up to 3,000 Open Craters along Coast Having Impact on Development," MSNBC, June 21, 2009, http://www.msnbc. msn.com/id/31475786/ns/world_news-environment/t/dead-sea-sinkholes-swallow-plans/#.UIaxW83D5IY.

Desert Survival Skills

David Alloway's book, *Desert Survival Skills* (Texas: University of Texas Press, 2000), is, as of this writing, still on Mark's bedside table and still available for purchase online.

The magazine article about Birthright Israel that I read following my trip is "The Romance of Birthright Israel: How US Funders and Israeli Politicians are Creating the Next Generation of American Zionists" by Kiera Feldman, *The Nation*, July 4, 2011, reported in partnership with The Investigative Fund at The Nation Institute, http://www.thenation.com/article/161460/romance-birthright-israel.

The op-ed article about Israeli kibbutzim and settlements is "Fictions on the Ground" by Tony Judt, *New York Times*, June 22, 2009, http://www.nytimes.com/2009/06/22/opinion/22judt.html?pagewanted=all.

The Salt Pillar of Lot's Wife

The news from the Palestinian village Bil'in about Israeli soldiers shooting high-powered tear-gas cannons into the crowd demonstrating against Israel's Separation Wall was reported in "Bil'in Weekly Demonstration," June 26, 2009, http://www.indybay.org/newsitems/2009/06/26/18604034.php. The death of a Palestinian man shot with one of those tear-gas cannons at a previous demonstration in Bil'in was noted in "Palestinians Urge Envoy to Press Israel on Statehood," *New York Times*, April 18, 2009, http://query.nytimes.com/gst/fullpage.html?res=9803EID71738F93BA25757C0A96F9C8B63.

The news about Jewish settlers raiding a Palestinian village near Nablus and Palestinians starting a fire at a nearby Jewish settlement was reported in "Israel to Build 50 New Homes at West Bank Settlement," *Reuters*, June 29, 2009, http://www.reuters.com/article/2009/06/29/us-palestinians-israel-settlements-idUSTRE55S1SP20090629.

Reports about Israeli soldiers preventing pro-Palestinian activists from helping Palestinian farmers in the Palestinian village Safa include: "Israeli Soldiers Scuffle with Activists in WBank," *Reuters*, June 27, 2009, http://www.reuters.com/article/2009/06/27/us-palestinians-israel-violence-idUSTRE55Q0OI20090627; and, "Unlikely Ally for Residents of West Bank," *New York Times*, June 28, 2009, http://www.nytimes.com/2009/06/22/opinion/22judt.html?sq=Palestinian&st=nyt&scp=34&pagewanted=print.

Go in Peace and Havahavahava Nice Day

News reports about Israel approving construction of fifty new homes in a Jewish settlement in the West Bank to accommodate the "natural growth" and opponents claiming the new homes were being built to entice Jewish immigrants from abroad to settle in the West Bank include: "Israel to Build 50 New Homes at West Bank Settlement," *Reuters*, June 29, 2009, http://www.reuters.com/article/2009/06/29/us-palestinians-israel-settlements-idUSTRE55SISP20090629; and, "Migrants Boost Jewish Settler Numbers in West Bank," *The Guardian*, June 24, 2009, http://www.guardian.co.uk/world/feedarticle/8574383.

The news about Jews "fueled by religious fervor" settling in the West Bank in areas not condoned by Israel is part of the NPR report "Activists Vow to Revive West Bank Settlement" by Lourdes Garcia-Navarro, which aired on June 29, 2009, http://www.npr.org/templates/story/story.php?storyId=106049895.

My source of information about the Jordan Valley of the West Bank and Israel's "de-facto" annexation was "Israel Has De Facto Annexed the Jordan Valley," B'Tselem, The Israeli Information Center for Human Rights in the Occupied Territories, February 13, 2006, http://www.btselem.org/settlements/20060213_annexation_of_the_jordan_valley. (Throughout this book, I refer to B'Tselem as "the Israeli human rights organization B'Tselem" or just "B'Tselem.")

I read several reports about Israeli bypass roads in the West Bank, including: "The Israeli Bypass Road System in the Occupied Palestinian Territory," Applied Research Institute Jerusalem, August 22, 2008, http://www.poica.org/editor/case_studies/

view.php?recordID=1513; and, "Forbidden Roads, Israel's Discriminatory Road Regime in the West Bank," B'Tselem, August 2004, http://www.btselem.org/download/200408_forbidden_roads_eng.pdf.

The news about the Israeli military preventing Palestinians from swimming at the Dead Sea beaches was reported in "Palestinians Barred from Dead Sea Beaches to 'Appease Israeli Settlers,'" *The Independent*, June 14, 2008, http://www.independent.co.uk/news/world/middle-east/palestinians-barred-from-dead-sea-beaches-to-appease-israeli-settlers-846948.html. I read about the group of Israeli women smuggling disguised Palestinian women through the Israeli checkpoint and into these beach areas in "Where Politics Are Complex, Simple Joys at the Beach," *New York Times*, July 26, 2011, http://www.nytimes.com/2011/07/27/world/middleeast/27swim.html?_r=0.

Wisdom is Like a Baobab

The news articles I read about the ultra-Orthodox codes of conduct, the schism between the ultra-Orthodox Jews and secular Jews, and the growing influence of the ultra-Orthodox on Israeli lifestyle include: "Orthodox Jewish 'Modesty Patrols' Put Israelis on Edge," *Fox News*, October 5, 2008, http://www.foxnews.com/story/0,2933,432876,00.html; "A Modern Marketplace for Israel's Ultra-Orthodox," *New York Times*, November 2, 2007, http://www.nytimes.com/2007/11/02/world/middleeast/02orthodox.html?pagewanted=all&_r=0; "Outrage as Jewish Newspapers Ban Pictures of Israel's New PM Because

She's a Woman," *Mail Online*, September 23, 2008, http://www.
dailymail.co.uk/news/article-1059789/Outrage-Jewish-newspa-
pers-ban-pictures-Israels-new-PM-shes-woman.html; "Haredim
to Continue Running Buses Segregating Men, Women," *Haaretz*,
March 22, 2009, http://www.haaretz.com/news/haredim-to-
continue-running-buses-segregating-men-women-1.272634; "A
Survey of Israel: A House of Many Mansions," *The Economist*, April
3, 2008, http://www.economist.com/node/10909900; "Haredi
Chutzpah," *Haaretz*, May 26, 2009, http://www.haaretz.com/
print-edition/opinion/haredi-chutzpah-1.276707; and, "Liber-
alism Has the Right to Defend Itself," *Haaretz*, January 1, 2009,
http://www.haaretz.com/print-edition/opinion/liberalism-has-
the-right-to-defend-itself-1.266819.

Jerusalem, al-Quds

On July 30, 1980, the Israeli Knesset passed the "Jerusalem Law"
proclaiming Jerusalem to be the capital of Israel. A copy of the
Jerusalem Law is available on the website of the Israel Ministry
of Foreign Affairs, http://www.mfa.gov.il/MFA/MFAAr-
chive/1980_1989/Basic%20Law-%20Jerusalem-%20Capi-
tal%20of%20Israel.

In response to Israel's proclamation that Jerusalem is the capital of Israel, on August 20, 1980, the UN Security Council unan-
imously adopted Resolution 478, condemning Israel's actions
as a violation of international law and declaring the Jerusalem
Law null and void; the resolution passed fourteen to zero with
the US abstaining. A copy of Resolution 478 is available on the

UNISPAL website, http://unispal.un.org/UNISPAL.NSF/0/
DDE590C6FF232007852560DF0065FDDB.

The news about the Israeli soldiers shooting and wound-
ing Palestinian children was reported in two articles that I read:
"Israeli Troops Wound Four Palestinians in West Bank," *Reuters*,
July 1, 2009, http://www.reuters.com/article/2009/07/01/
us-palestinians-israel-violence-sb-idUSTRE5604ZE20090701;
and, "Israel: Court Orders Stiffer Charges in Shooting," *New York
Times*, July 2, 2009, http://www.nytimes.com/2009/07/02/
world/middleeast/02briefs-israelmilitary.html.

Here, of the Virgin Mary, Jesus Christ Was Born

On June 27, 1967, just days following the Six-Day War, Israel "unilaterally annexed" an area on the West Bank side of the Green Line
that included Jerusalem's Old City, East Jerusalem, and an additional
sixty-four square kilometers that belonged to twenty-eight Palestinian villages. The annexation ordinances are available on the website of
the Israel Ministry of Foreign Affairs, http://www.mfa.gov.il/MFA/
Foreign+Relations/Israels+Foreign+Relations+since+1947/1947-
1974/13+Law+and+Administration+Ordinance+-
Amendment+No.htm.

In response to Israel's attempt to annex the area on the West
Bank side of the Green Line that included Jerusalem's Old City,
East Jerusalem, and the additional sixty-four square kilometers
that belonged to twenty-eight Palestinian villages, the UN Security
Council, on November 22, 1967, adopted Resolution 242, call-
ing for Israel's withdrawal from the unilaterally annexed areas and

all other areas in the Palestinian territories. A copy of Resolution 242 is available on the UNISPAL website, http://unispal.un.org/unispal.nsf/0/7D35E1F729DF491C85256EE700686136.

The statistics for average net daily wages for males, percentage of households below poverty line, and hotel occupancy rates are just a few of those that were prepared by the Palestinian Central Bureau of Statistics and reprinted in the booklet *This Week in Palestine*, Issue No. 135 (July 2009), pp. 88-89 (the quote about the Israeli Separation Wall serving as a backdrop for Palestinian fashion shows and other cultural events is on page 3 of that issue).

Come and Celebrate Palestine

Much of what Mark shared with me about the Palestinian peaceful resistance movement in Beit Sahour he had read on the Beit Sahour website, http://www.beitsahourmunicipality.com/english/historic.htm.

When I returned home, I discovered a *New York Times* news article about the tax resistance movement in Beit Sahour: "Abroad at Home: It Can Happen There," October 29, 1989, http://www.nytimes.com/1989/10/29/opinion/abroad-at-home-it-can-happen-there.html.

For more information supporting George's opinion that Israel is "wiping historic Palestine off the map" and using tourism as a political tool by imposing restrictions on Palestinian tour operators, see the Siraj Center website, http://www.sirajcenter.org/index.php?option=com_content&task=view&id=137&Ite

mid=72, and the Beit Sahour website, http://www.beitsahour-municipality.com/english/historic.htm.

George mentioned that West Bank Palestinians must register with the Israeli government. I later learned more about this: Israel requires Palestinian families to register children at birth. Apparently, many families failed to register their children at birth, and Israel refused late registration for these children. Unregistered children have no legal status and aren't eligible for the official Israeli-issued identification card, which Israel requires Palestinians to carry at all times. The identification card is necessary to show proof of identity and to obtain full access to basic things like education and medical care. Unregistered Palestinians face daily and lifelong discrimination. The Israeli human rights organization B'Tselem concluded that Israel's refusal to issue identification cards to unregistered Palestinians, which leaves them in a state of limbo with no legal status, is a violation of international law and a humanitarian crisis. One unregistered Palestinian interviewed by B'Tselem said: "I long for the day I'll finally get an ID card. I want to pass through each and every checkpoint in the West Bank, just to show everyone I have an ID card. Sometimes I feel that death will be the only solution to my problem. In the afterlife I'm sure no one gets asked about his ID card." "Israel Refuses to Issue ID Cards to Unregistered Palestinians," B'Tselem, May 29, 2008, http://www.btselem.org/family_separation/20080529_unregistered_persons.

George's comments about travel restrictions in the West Bank are true. According to B'Tselem, Israel's web of restrictions *within* the West Bank included forty-seven checkpoints, more than four hundred physical obstructions on roads, and the Separation Wall, 80 percent of which was located *inside* the West Bank; in addition, Israel prohibited or restricted vehicles with Palestinian license plates from traveling on over three hundred kilometers of main roads in the West Bank. The restrictions effectively split the West Bank into six separate geographic areas, B'Tselem concluded. "The restrictions impede access to medical services. The difficulty in getting to work, the constant lack of certainty, and the greater expenses resulting from the restrictions gravely affect the economy and trade in the West Bank. The restrictions impair family and social ties. Other negative ramifications include a decline in the supply of infrastructure services and in law enforcement in areas under the responsibility of the Palestinian Authority." B'Tselem called on Israeli government and military to remove all permanent restrictions on movement within the West Bank and to concentrate security efforts along the Green Line or inside Israel. "For Seven Years, Israel Has Denied Palestinians Freedom of Movement to Ease Travel for Israelis in the West Bank," B'Tselem, August 2007, http://www.btselem.org/press_releases/20070807.

Numerous news articles I read substantiated George's claims about the "man-made drought" in the West Bank, including: "Israel Rations Palestinians to Trickle of Water," Amnesty International, October 27, 2009, http://www.amnesty.org/en/news-and-updates/report/israel-rations-palestinians-trickle-water-20091027; "Israelis Get Four-Fifths of Scarce West Bank Water, Says World Bank" *The Guardian*, May 27, 2009, http://www.guardian.co.uk/world/2009/may/27/israel-palestinian-water-dispute; "Water Shortage Cripples

Palestinian Farming," *Reuters*, September 18, 2008, http://
www.reuters.com/article/2008/09/18/us-palestinians-water-
idUSLA43722220080918; and, "B'Tselem Warns of Grave
Water Shortage in the West Bank: Average Water Consumption
in Israel is 3.5 Times That in West Bank," B'Tselem, July 1, 2008,
http://www.btselem.org/water/2008070_acute_water_short-
age_in_the_west_bank. For a detailed report on the restrictions
on Palestinian development of water resources and the economic,
social, and environmental impact of those restrictions, see the
World Bank's comprehensive research report "West Bank and
Gaza: Assessment of Restrictions on Palestinian Water Sector
Development," The World Bank Sector Note, April 2009, http://
water.worldbank.org/node/83738.

For information supporting George's comment that "Israel
is using water as a tool of harassment, as a tool of displacement, making your life so miserable that you want to leave," see
the 162-page Human Rights Watch research report "Separate
and Unequal: Israel's Discriminatory Treatment of Palestinians
in the Occupied Palestinian Territories," Human Rights Watch,
December 2010, http://www.hrw.org/reports/2010/12/19/
separate-and-unequal-0.

Closed Military Zones and Flying Checkpoints

The news about Israeli soldiers cordoning off the Palestinian farm
at Safa and kicking out Palestinian and International activists was
covered in two news articles: "Israeli Soldiers Scuffle with Activists in WBank," *Reuters*, June 27, 2009, http://www.reuters.com/

article/2009/06/27/us-palestinians-israel-violence-idUS-TRE55Q0OI20090627; and, "Unlikely Ally for Residents of West Bank," *New York Times*, June 28, 2009, http://www.nytimes.com/2009/06/22/opinion/22judt.html?sq=Palestinian&st=nyt&scp=34&pagewanted=print.

I read a United Nations report that confirmed Beckah's statement about the Israeli military obstructing Palestinian access to land then declaring the land abandoned and requisitioning it for Jewish settlements. According to the report, over one-fifth of the land in the West Bank had been closed by the Israeli military for "military purposes." See, "The Humanitarian Impact on Palestinians of Israeli Settlements and Other Infrastructure in the West Bank," UN Office for the Coordination of Humanitarian Affairs (OCHA) (July 2007), pp. 42-43, http://unispal.un.org/UNISPAL.NSF/0/E6BAF87B060A607085257347006F3FAF.

The Israeli settlements in the West Bank are illegal under international law. According to the Israeli human rights organization B'Tselem: "International humanitarian law prohibits the occupying power to transfer citizens from its own territory to the occupied territory (Fourth Geneva Convention, article 49). The Hague Regulations prohibit the occupying power to undertake permanent changes in the occupied area, unless these are due to military needs in the narrow sense of the term, or unless they are undertaken for the benefit of the local population. The establishment of the settlements leads to the violation of the rights of the Palestinians as enshrined in international human rights law. Among other violations, the settlements infringe the right to self-determination, equality, property, an adequate standard of living, and freedom of movement." "Land Grab: Israel's Settlement Policy in the West Bank, May 2002," http://www.btselem.org/publications/summaries/200205_land_grab. For more information, including Israel's countering arguments, see chapter two of the full report, "The Settlements in International Law," http://www.btselem.org/sites/default/files/publication/200205_land_grab_eng.pdf.

Stink Water and Nasty Graffiti

Benny Morris writes about the exodus of Arabs from areas that fell to Israel and into Hebron and other areas in the West Bank in *1948 and After*, p. 104.

One of numerous news reports I read about Baruch Goldstein's massacre is "Massacre at the Mosque," *The Guardian*, February 26, 1994, http://www.guardian.co.uk/theguardian/2010/jun/08/archive-massacre-at-mosque-1994.

Sandy Tolan discusses some of the repercussions of the Goldstein massacre in his book *The Lemon Tree*, p. 227: "Six weeks later after Goldstein massacre, Hamas, the militant Islamic organization, abandoned its strategy of attacking only Israeli military targets. On April 6, a car bomb exploded in the Israeli town of Afula, killing six Israeli civilians. A communique declared that the attack was revenge for those who died in the Hebron massacre. The cycle of pain and retaliation had returned. Suicide bombers recruited by Hamas blew themselves up in Netanya, Hadera, Jerusalem, Tel Aviv, and occupied portions of the Gaza strip, killing dozens of Israelis. Hamas leaders claimed each attack on civilians was direct response to Israeli attacks that killed Palestinian civilians."

A copy of the 1997 Hebron Protocol, which divided Hebron into H-1 and H-2, is available on the UNISPAL website, http://unispal.un.org/UNISPAL.NSF/0/C7D7B824004FF-5C585256AE700543EBC.

The Israeli human rights organization B'Tselem, as part of its camera distribution project, gave video recorders to Palestinians living in high conflict areas in the West Bank so they could record the reality of their life under the Israeli occupation. You can read more about the camera distribution project—and watch the videos taken by Palestinian families—on the B'Tselem website, http://www.btselem.org/video/cdp_background.

In addition to the videos posted on the B'Tselem website, I discovered dozens of videos on YouTube taken in Hebron by Tel Rumeida's Palestinian residents documenting abuse by Jewish settlers. See, for example, http://www.youtube.com/watch?v=kem1ajIKvIk.

Attacks on and abuse of Hebron's Palestinian residents by both Jewish settlers and Israeli soldiers is well documented. According to B'Tselem: "Over the years, settlers in the city have routinely abused the city's Palestinian residents, sometimes using extreme violence. Throughout the second intifada, settlers have committed physical assaults, including beatings, at times with clubs, stone throwing, and hurling of refuse, sand, water, chlorine, and empty bottles. Settlers have destroyed shops and doors, committed thefts, and chopped down fruit trees. Settlers have also been involved in gunfire, attempts to run people over, poisoning of a water well, breaking into homes, spilling of hot liquid on the face of a Palestinian, and the killing of a young Palestinian girl.

Soldiers are generally positioned on every street corner in and near the settlement points, but in most cases they do nothing to protect Palestinians from the settlers' attacks." "Ghost Town: Israel's Separation Policy and Forced Eviction of Palestinians from the Center of Hebron," B'Tselem, May 2007, http://www.btselem. org/publications/summaries/200705_hebron.

Many former Israeli soldiers have admitted to intentionally and systematically abusing Hebron's Palestinian residents. Testimonies and videos of these soldiers and others are available on the website of Breaking the Silence, an Israeli nongovernmental organization formed by former Israeli soldiers stationed in Hebron for the purpose of exposing this abuse, http://www.breakingthesilence.org.il/about/organization. I read numerous news articles about Breaking the Silence, including: "Our Reign of Rerror, by the Israeli Army: In Shocking Testimonies that Reveal Abductions, Beatings and Torture, Israeli Soldiers Confess the Horror They Have Visited on Hebron," *The Independent*, April 19, 2008, http://www. independent.co.uk/news/world/middle-east/our-reign-of-terror-by-the-israeli-army-811769.html; and, "Mario Vargas Llosa: How Arabs Have Been Driven Out of Hebron," *The Independent*, April 19, 2008, http://www.independent.co.uk/voices/commentators/mario-vargas-llosa-how-arabs-have-been-driven-out-of-hebron-811770.html.

Baruch Marzel, the former Kach member who lives in the compound overlooking the Al-Azzehs' yard, has a long Israeli criminal record for assaulting Palestinians. At the time I was in Hebron, he was head of the right wing Zionist Jewish National Front.

After Nisreen told me about Israeli soldiers preventing her from going to a hospital to give birth, I read more about the commonplace practice at Israeli checkpoints in the study "Checkpoints Compound the Risks of Childbirth for Palestinian Women," United Nations Population Fund, May 15, 2007, http://www.unfpa.org/public/site/global/News/pid/310.

When I returned to Austin, I discovered on YouTube a video of the Jewish settlers of Tel Rumeida attempting to prevent Nisreen's husband, Hasheem Al-Azzeh, from harvesting his olives: http://www.youtube.com/watch?v=JMA3baJa6tg.

The Israeli human rights organization B'Tselem study concluding that Israeli forces, in the process of protecting the Jewish settlers of Hebron, had caused the economic collapse of the entire city center is "Ghost Town: Israel's Separation Policy and Forced Eviction of Palestinians from the Center of Hebron," B'Tselem, May 2007, http://www.btselem.org/publications/summaries/200705_hebron. According to B'Tselem: "The Israeli settlement points in Hebron, which were established in breach of Israel's obligations under international law, cause severe and continuous breaches of international legal provisions intended to protect the human rights of persons under belligerent occupation. Israel contends that it is impossible to ensure the safety of the settlers without separating Palestinians and Israelis in the city, and without infringing the basic rights of the Palestinian residents, which has resulted in Palestinians leaving the City Center. The State of Israel has the legal and moral obligation to evacuate the Israelis who settled in Hebron and bring them back to Israel," http://www.btselem.org/hebron.

For more information on the Israeli occupation of Hebron and the humanitarian and economic effect of the Israeli occupation, see "The Palestinian Life inside the Old City of Hebron," Applied Research Institute Jerusalem, September 27, 2005, http://www.poica.org/editor/case_studies/view.php?recordID=670.

Shabbat Desecraters Must Die!

I read about the ultra-Orthodox protestors setting trash cans on fire in the news article "Haredi Protesters: Shabbat Desecraters Must Die!" *The Jerusalem Post*, July 5, 2009. The letter to the editor expressing a different point of view is in the same paper.

Refugee Rappers

For more information on the birth of the Palestinian refugee problem, see "The Harvest of 1948 and the Creation of the Palestinian Refugee Problem," in Benny Morris's book *1948 and After*, pp. 339-256.

By December 1948, hundreds of thousands of refugees fled or were forced out of areas captured by Israel. On December 11, 1948, the UN General Assembly passed Resolution194 (III), which stated that "refugees wishing to return to their homes and live at peace with their neighbors should be permitted to do so at the earliest practicable date, and that compensation should be paid for the property of those choosing not to return." A copy of Resolution 194 is available on the UNISPAL website, http://unispal.un.org/UNISPAL.NSF/0/C758572B78D1CD-0085256BCF0077E51A.

Israeli forces barred reentry of the refugees and destroyed hundreds of Palestinian villages and repopulated others with immigrants from Eastern Europe. Sandy Tolan, in his book *The Lemon Tree*, tells the story of an Arab (Palestinian) family that fled their home in an Israeli-captured area during the summer of 1948, and a Jewish family who arrived from Eastern Europe a few months later and were given the home by the Israeli government—the Israeli government "had declared itself the 'custodian' of the houses it considered abandoned property," p. 105. For a collection of firsthand accounts of the Nakba, see "Voices of the Nakba, 1948—2008," *Washington Report on Middle East Affairs*, Volume XXVII, No. 4, May/June 2008, http://www.washington-report. org/archives/235-washington-report-archives-2006-2010/may-june-2008.html.

Israel refused to comply with UN Resolution 194, which gave Palestinian refugees the right to return to their home villages in areas captured by Israel, and the UN lacked power to enforce the resolution. On December 8, 1949, in the absence of any other solution, the UN General Assembly passed Resolution 302 (IV), which created the UN Relief and Works Agency for Palestine Refugees in the Near East (UNRWA) to provide housing, assistance, and programs for the refugees. A copy of Resolution 302 is available on the UNISPAL website, http://unispal.un.org/UNI-SPAL.NSF/0/AF5F909791DE7FB0852560E500687282. More information about UNRWA is available on the agency's website, http://www.unrwa.org/index.php.

In his book *Wall and Peace*, the British graffiti artist Banksy stated: "Palestine has been occupied by the Israeli army since

1967. In 2002 the Israeli government began building a wall separating the occupied territories from Israel, much of it illegal under international law. It is controlled by a series of checkpoints and observation towers, stands three times the height of the Berlin Wall and will eventually run for over 700km—the distance from London to Zurich. Palestine is now the world's largest open-air prison and the ultimate activity holiday destination for graffiti artists." Banksy, *Wall and Peace* (United Kingdom: Century 2006), p. 136.

I found a news article about the boy Shadi told us about—the boy who went left Dheisheh to purchase a bag of concrete mix for his father and was mistakenly shot by Israeli soldiers. According to the article, "Qusay Al-Afandi, a seventeen year-old from Duheisha Refugee Camp, died from bullet wounds sustained in clashes between Palestinian youths and Israeli military forces," "Funeral of Palestinian Teenager Killed by Israeli Forces in Bethlehem," Ma'an News Agency, January 28, 2008, http://www.maannews.net/eng/ViewDetails.aspx?ID=200883. The camp name is spelled many different ways in English, even on buildings within the camp.

The statistics for fatalities between December1987 and January 2009 (7,863 Palestinians killed by Israelis; 1,493 Israelis killed by Palestinians) came from the B'Tselem reports "Fatalities in the First Intifada," "Fatalities Since the Outbreak of the Second Intifada and Until Operation 'Cast Lead,'" and "Fatalities during operation 'Cast Lead,'" http://www.btselem.org/statistics. The reports did not specify which fatalities were the result of suicide bombings. A list of all suicide and other bombing attacks in Israel since 1993 is available on The Israel Ministry of Foreign Affairs website, http://www.mfa.gov.il/MFA/Terrorism-+Obstacle+to+Peace/Palestinian+terror+since+2000/Suicide+and+Other+Bombing+Attacks+in+Israel+Since.htm.

Several articles I read confirmed what Shadi said about Palestinians feeling proud of family members and friends who undertook suicide strikes against Israelis. Michael Finkel, in his December 2005 *National Geographic* article "Bethlehem," quoted a twenty-eight-year-old Dheisheh resident saying of his friend who was a suicide bomber, "I'm proud of him. . . . He did something great. The Israelis have forced us into this situation. They have left us with nothing. And when you have nothing, you have nothing to lose," http://ngm.nationalgeographic.com/ngm/2007-12/bethlehem/finkel-text-p7.html. Another article I read was about a fifty-seven-year-old woman with nine children and nearly thirty grandchildren who detonated a suicide device, killing herself and injuring several Israeli soldiers; her son was quoted as saying, "I am very proud of what she did," "Grandmother Attempts Suicide Bombing in Gaza," *IOL News*, November 24, 2006, http://www.iol.co.za/news/world/grandmother-attempts-suicide-bombing-in-gaza-1.304633#.UJFsHM3kW3c.

The Ibdaa Cultural Center at the Dheisheh Refugee Camp has a website with photographs and information, http://www.dheisheh-ibdaa.net/home.htm, though each time I accessed the website from my home computer all of the text had been mysteriously blocked out.

Thou Shalt Not Steal

For more information on Beit Jala, as well as Israel's confiscation of the village's land, see the Beit Jala website, http://www.beit-jala-city.org/en/beit-jala-city/history-culture. See also "Walling In the Bethlehem Ghetto: Beit Jala Land Seizure," April 21, 2004, Applied Research Institute Jerusalem, http://www.poica.org/editor/case_studies/view.php?recordID=368.

Israel has taken control of over half the land in the West Bank mainly for establishing and expanding Israeli settlements, and the mechanism most often employed was declaring land "state land," according to the Israeli human rights organization B'Tselem. "Using a complex legal-bureaucratic mechanism, Israel took control of some 50 percent of the land of the West Bank, primarily for establishment of the settlements and preparation of land reserves for their expansion. The main means used for this purpose is declaring and recording the land as 'state land.' The process employed in taking control of land breaches the basic principles of due procedure and natural justice. In many cases, Palestinian residents were unaware that their land was registered in the name of the state, and by the time they discovered this fact, it was too late to appeal. The burden of proof always rests with the Palestinian claiming ownership of the land. Even if he meets this burden, the land may still be registered in the name of the state on the grounds that it was transferred to the settlement 'in good faith.'. . . The legal cloak that Israel has used as a cover for the settlement enterprise is aimed at concealing the continuing theft of land in the West Bank," http://www.btselem.org/settlements/taking_control. See also "Access Denied: Israeli Measures to Deny

Palestinians Access to Land Around Settlement," B'Tselem, p.17, September 2008, http://www.btselem.org/download/200809_access_denied_eng.pdf.

More information about the Tent of Nations is available on its website, http://www.tentofnations.org/, and on the website of Friends of the Tent of Nations, http://fotonna.org/.

On May 27, 2010, less than a year after Mark and I visited the Tent of Nations, Daoud Nassar, the Christian Palestinian who formed the Tent of Nations to protect his family's farm from confiscation by the Israeli military, sent this urgent letter to his friends and supporters:

Dear Friends of Tent of Nations all over the world:

Today at 2.00 pm in the afternoon, two officers from the Israeli Civil Administration guarded by Israeli soldiers came to our farm and gave us NINE demolishing orders for nine (structures) we built in the last years without a building permit from the Israeli Military Authority. The demolishing orders are for: tents, animals shelters, metal roof in front of both old houses, the restrooms (Shelters), a water cistern, a metal container and two underground renovated cave structures. One officer was writing the demolishing orders and the other was taking pictures with two cameras, Israeli soldiers were following them everywhere and pointing their guns on us.

The demolishing orders were written in Hebrew and I refused to sign receiving them. We have three days only to react against those demolishing orders. The timing for delivering the demolishing orders was planned properly and purposely on Thursday, in order to make it difficult for us to try to stop those orders by the Israeli court within three days, because of the Jewish weekend (Friday and

Saturday). The idea is to make it impossible for us to act quickly. I contacted our lawyer and he will write an opposition and send it to the military court on Sunday morning. We hope to get a paper from the court through our lawyer on Sunday morning to stop the demolishing orders.

We would like to ask you to be prepared and alert for actions, if anything might happen. We will keep you updated and will guide you for actions but please forward this email to your friends.

PLEASE be prepared for actions. Thank you for all your solidarity and support.

They are trying to destroy our spirit, but we are determined to resist and overcome the Evil with GOOD and justice will prevail.

Blessings and Salaam,
Daoud

Made in the USA
Charleston, SC
22 March 2013